*Developing Successful
College Writing Programs*

Edward M. White

Foreword by Richard Lloyd-Jones

Developing Successful
College Writing Programs

Jossey-Bass Publishers

San Francisco   •   London   •   1989

DEVELOPING SUCCESSFUL COLLEGE WRITING PROGRAMS
by Edward M. White

Copyright © 1989 by: Jossey-Bass Inc., Publishers
350 Sansome Street
San Francisco, California 94104
&
Jossey-Bass Limited
28 Banner Street
London EC1Y 8QE

Library of Congress Cataloging-in-Publication Data

White, Edward M. (Edward Michael), date.
    Developing successful college writing programs / Edward M. White;
foreword by Richard Lloyd-Jones.
        p.   cm.—(The Jossey-Bass higher education series)
    Bibliography: p.
    Includes index.
    ISBN 1-55542-131-8
    1. English language—Rhetoric—Study and teaching. (Higher)
I. Title. II. Series.
PE1404.W47   1989
808'.042'0711—dc19   88-30416
                                                           CIP

Manufactured in the United States of America

JACKET DESIGN BY WILLI BAUM

FIRST EDITION

Code 8904

The Jossey-Bass
Higher Education Series

Consulting Editor
Teaching and Learning

Kenneth E. Eble
University of Utah

Contents

Foreword

Because writing and reading underlie all school learning, some people assume that instruction in these subjects is elementary as well as basic. Because basic instruction sometimes follows patterns established at least two and a half millennia ago, some people assume that nothing new needs to be learned about writing. Because college students vary widely in the elements of language they control, mass instruction is often wasteful; but tutoring or small-group instruction, although actually efficient, appears to many as merely "remedial" or "covering what they should have learned before" and thus seems a threat to "standards" as well as an unnecessary expense. Teachers of such students are sometimes perceived as "social workers" or "support personnel" rather than as "real faculty."

On the other hand, almost everyone gives at least lip service to the importance of writing, especially if someone else can be blamed for poor performance. Even those who accept arguments for writing-across-the-curriculum programs sometimes do not recognize the degree to which the definition of good writing may be specific to a given field. English professors, sociology professors, and chemistry professors do not always recognize the same virtues. Often all of them, being fluent themselves in their own dialects, underestimate the complexity of composition, at least until they have to respond to student papers, at which time they complain about the work involved and damn the ignorance of youth. Chapter One of this book, in describing the campus climate for writing, offers additional documentation for this point.

In short, most college faculties and their administrators need advice about providing useful help to the writing programs. Because few of the people assigned to administer such programs really have much appropriate background before they start, writing program administrators also need advice. Into this void comes Edward M. White, a literary scholar who served a stint as a departmental administrator. During his term as department chair, he found himself in the midst of California's efforts to assess the writing of students being admitted to the state university system and to judge the usefulness of the college-level writing programs. What began as a large committee assignment in response to public demands became more than a decade of test designing, program describing, and practical administration, mostly with the aid of federal and state grants. The novels of Jane Austen, literary criticism, and the contemplative life of the scholar were put aside so that White could become a master of what has often been ignored because of the assumption that "everyone knows." Chapter Two of this book, the one describing other studies of writing programs, suggests how necessary this book is. Almost nothing about writing program administration is otherwise available in an accessible form.

The remaining chapter of the first section exhibits another aspect of the problem—namely, that most of the basic terms, although part of everyone's vocabulary, are equivocal and elusive. Even the term *writing* invites misunderstanding. Library references often turn out to deal with handwriting. Some people are really talking about preparation of manuscripts. Others refer to academic conventions or social signaling. Still others use the term to refer to all discourse. And there are other meanings. Discussion bounces back and forth without clear distinctions among competing vocabularies; so research under one heading is used to support notions that really belong under another heading. Ordinary status reports about different programs are suspect because rarely are data collected in parallel ways. By describing current approaches to instruction at various levels and by commenting on techniques for measuring writing ability (or describing style) as he does in Chapters Four and Five, White attempts to make discussion more orderly and thus provides a framework for negotiating decisions about local programs.

Chapters Six and Seven deal with common organizational challenges. Every student comes to college quite adept at some writing skills, but colleges have to discover which ones and find for each writer a class with suitable instruction. Every teacher is really a writing coach and invites the class to become collaborators in editing proposed texts written by students in the class. Ultimately, writing is judged in terms of its social effectiveness even though composition is a solitary act. All good assignments exist in tension between constraints as defined by the instructor and the freedom of imagining particular solutions within the students' worlds. "Open" should mean "adaptive to individual needs and experiences," not "anything goes." Similarly, "revision" should mean "re-seeing" and thus encourage more than editing. Possibly the best revision assignments deal with writing on the "same" topic for different audiences or different purposes or different frames of reference. White defines the questions that administrators must ask in order to set useful goals, and he surveys different kinds of solutions in different contexts. These chapters provide concrete examples and arguments for making the decisions required to address the issues described in the first five chapters.

The final three chapters emphasize that immediate policies have long-range implications, especially in sustaining an appropriate faculty both at the college level and in the schools. If colleges are inept in teaching writing, they probably will send inept teachers to the schools—teachers who thus neglect the function of language in all learning and social relationships. Fortunately, most students who enroll in college have learned to use the language in practice, and often the educational system merely rewards those who are fortunate enough to grow up in a suitable environment, but the good luck of that privileged group does not free colleges and schools from the responsibility to enhance the verbal powers of all students. And since that goal is so important, it is proper that programs devise ways to demonstrate their effectiveness in achieving what they aspire to. Claims that a program is successful often seem merely to reflect an administrative desire to avoid more discussion on the subject.

In an age of nostrums, it would be easy to buy into easy solutions. Many of the popular prescriptions about writing simply offer another example of our flight from complexity, of the desire to "solve" difficult problems by pretending that no problem exists or by offering a cheap formula. White concentrates on providing information that will allow administrators to understand challenges to learning so fundamental that they define learning itself. Possibly no program can ever fully meet the challenge, but neither can any respectable college evade always trying to do a better job.

November 1988   Richard Lloyd-Jones
                                               Department of English
                                               University of Iowa

Preface

Developing Successful College Writing Programs began with a perception and a question. Those who evaluate campus programs recognize that some institutions have more effective writing programs than others, but they do not know the root causes of these differences or why apparently similar programs work well in some cases and not in others. A small group of faculty from different campuses in the California State University (CSU) system began discussing these matters in the late 1970s, wondering whether we could discover some general principles and key components that are typical of the most effective programs. In 1980, we persuaded the (then) National Institute of Education to provide funding for an extended inquiry into the question, using the nineteen-campus CSU as a kind of laboratory. That study continued for five years, leading to a two-volume report (White and Polin, 1986) that answered some questions and raised many more. This book is only indirectly related to that research project. The questions about writing program effectiveness that lay behind those five years of research are, however, the informing ones behind this book.

The literature on writing programs is surprisingly small, though there is a never-ending supply of books purporting to teach students how to write or to teach teachers how to help students learn. Those responsible for or concerned about institutional writing programs have been able to consult a few, largely descriptive, studies (see Chapter Two), but this book is the first attempt to include a background of program research, a discussion of program issues, and practical applications and recommendations in a single volume. I make no attempt to hide my own strong opinions in the book, but these opinions have been shaped by thirty years of college-level teaching and more than a decade of administration of writing programs at the course, campus, and system-wide level; to this experience I have tried to add the insights and discoveries of recent writing research, as well as my own theoretical concerns as the principal investigator of a particular research project. I have also profited greatly from exchanges of ideas and manuscripts with my colleagues in the California State University English Council, the National Testing Network in Writing (centered at the City University of New York), the National Council of Writing Program Administrators, and the Conference on College Composition and Communication. American higher education has a wonderful variety of institutions, and I have tried to construct this book so that it would be of value to the local situation.

While the book is specifically directed at those concerned with the administration or direction of writing programs, it ought also to be of interest to those who teach in those programs. Many writing teachers wind up directing programs at some point in their careers, and even those who do not will find that the issues in this book touch on their daily working lives. I approach organizational concerns as a teacher, and I approach writing research as a writer as well as a researcher; many of the chapters speak specifically to such matters as approaches to the teaching of writing, the role of assessment in teaching, and the institutional reward structure for writing teachers. These concerns affect all faculty, not only those who teach writing, and will, I hope, be of interest to a wide range of college teachers and administrators. As I conduct more and more faculty seminars in writing across the curriculum, I become more and more convinced that concern about the role of writing and writing programs is wide and deep in the professoriate. If the ability to think and write is central to a liberal arts education, as most educated people will agree, this book speaks to anyone concerned with the practice and directions of American higher education.

The State of Writing Programs Today

Writing instruction programs have become particularly important to American colleges and universities in recent years for several reasons: a new awareness of the central importance of writing to critical thinking; a rebirth of interest in active rather than passive learning; an increasing attempt to include among the student body groups of students who may be without traditional training in reading and writing skills; technological advances that promise new methods of teaching and writing; and a major advance in disciplinary self-consciousness on the part of writing specialists, who have been conducting and publishing research in the field at a dizzying pace. In addition, assessment issues at all levels, including "value-added" testing for courses and writing proficiency testing for college graduates, have put increased pressure on institutions to improve the quality of their instructional and support programs.

Yet college and university writing programs usually develop organically as needs appear; they are not so much planned or organized as inherited and casually coordinated. On most campuses, the separate activities and courses relating to composition are not even conceived of as a writing program. The English department will have developed a freshman course or a series of courses in composition; the study skills center may have some writing tutorial programs and a computer drill package or two; the testing office may administer some tests for placement or proficiency in writing; the education department might include writing in its methods courses for future English teachers, or give writing tests of its own, or even offer study skills courses for entering freshmen. Often, special programs, such as writing-across-the-curriculum workshops for faculty or tutorials for students admitted under special status, appear and disappear according to soft money grants or the interests of particular faculty or academic vice-presidents. Administrators of parts of the writing program rarely talk to one another, and budget competition is much more common than cooperation.

Many campus administrators simply assume that writing is the business of the English department, although they are aware that most college English departments are primarily concerned with the study of literature. Many English departments have appointed a writing program administrator (WPA) to oversee the demanding freshman writing program, and they assume that the WPA is keeping an eye out for all writing instruction and related programs at the institution. The WPA, often with low status and a crushing work load, in turn assumes that someone higher in the administrative chain is attending to institutional matters out of his or her purview. When asked, every administrator will acknowledge the importance of writing and the buried existence of an extensive writing program on campus; that program is, however, usually someone else's responsibility, or nobody's.

This book seeks to focus attention on postsecondary writing programs as wide ranging and complex, demanding special concern from faculty and administration. Since writing and the critical thinking it requires are central to the idea of liberal education, institutions serious about the education they provide should review carefully the various aspects of writing instruction as they appear (or ought to appear) on campus and throughout the curriculum. Administration of and responsibility for writing programs should be considered and decided upon, not left to chance or tradition. The basic purpose of *Developing Successful College Writing Programs* is to set out the theoretical and practical issues that can lead to decisions that are appropriate to the individual campus situation.

The Contents of This Book

The first three chapters of the book examine the current status of writing instruction. Chapter One stipulates a definition of writing as centrally concerned with thought, as well as with expression, and relates that definition to the goals of

American higher education. Chapter Two reviews the slim literature about writing programs, and Chapter Three assesses the implications of that literature for the classroom teaching of writing.

The next three chapters look at practical ways to provide a basis for effective writing programs. Chapter Four is concerned with what happens in the writing classroom, considering particularly the relation of writing instruction to the undergraduate curriculum; this chapter looks closely at the characteristics of effective and ineffective writing courses. Chapter Five focuses on the assessment of writing ability and the relation of that assessment to teaching. Chapter Six considers the assessment of writing ability as it applies to the entire writing program, from admission and placement through exit-level requirements.

The last four chapters shift perspective somewhat to an organizational level. Chapter Seven looks at the entire writing program, examining its various existing and potential components as part of a comprehensive institutional approach to individual student learning. Chapter Eight focuses on institutional treatment of writing program faculty and administrators; Chapter Nine looks at college and university responsibility for the training of school writing teachers and for assisting the schools in which they teach; and Chapter Ten concludes the book with an examination of the vexing problem of evaluating the effectiveness of writing programs. The resources at the back of the book include an innovative evaluation research design and the self-study document prepared by the Council of Writing Program Administrators.

The reference section is selective rather than comprehensive and is designed for those who wish to pursue the educational and organizational concerns of this book. Much of the material cited is very recent. The vitality of writing research in general was brought home to me as the manuscript was going through revision: no less than five significant volumes (not to speak of many important journal articles) appeared, and demanded inclusion, after this book was in second draft (Hartzog, 1986; Hillocks, 1986; North, 1987; Tate, 1987; Ruth and Murphy, 1988).

Acknowledgments

I owe a particular debt to the research team of CSU English faculty that assisted in all aspects of the 1980–1985 NIE research project: Kim Flachmann, Charles Moore, David Rankin, and William Stryker. So many of the ideas in this book originated in spirited discussion with this team that I am unable to distinguish who said what; I have incorporated what I learned from these colleagues and friends silently into my own thinking and into this book. Linda Polin, now of Pepperdine University, worked as assistant director of the project for much of its life; to her I am indebted for the table reproduced in Chapter Three and all the statistical expertness that it represents. She was also responsible for an early draft of the literature review that has been transformed into Chapter Two.

Most of Chapter Ten and portions of Chapters Nine and Five were initially prepared as talks to conferences of the National Testing Network in Writing (NTNW). I am grateful to Karen Greenberg and her fellow directors of the NTNW for the stimulation they have provided for creative thinking about the role of writing measurement in American colleges and universities.

Kenneth Eble has been a steady, severe, and constructive critic of the manuscript as it has developed over several years. I owe to him what all of us owe to the best writing teachers we have encountered—that is, deep gratitude for refusing to accept less than our best efforts. His advice on organizing and deleting has been particularly valuable. I also thank Lynn Z. Bloom for a detailed and responsive reading of a draft, which led to yet more valuable revision.

San Bernardino, California   Edward M. White
November 1988

The Author

Edward M. White is professor and former chair of the Department of English at the California State University, San Bernardino. He received his B.A. degree (1955) from New York University and both his M.A. (1956) and Ph.D. (1960) degrees from Harvard University, focusing on literature.

Since 1970, when White published his first freshman composition textbook, his major research concern has been the teaching of writing. In 1972, he was appointed the first director of the California State University (CSU) Freshman English Equivalency Examination, a position he held through 1983. During those years, he served the nineteen-campus CSU in several additional capacities, coordinating system-wide activities in credit by examination, in the development of an English placement test, in the implementation of an upper-division writing requirement for degree recipients, and in overall administration of its writing skills improvement program.

White has given many workshops on measurement, the improvement of teaching, and writing across the curriculum for such institutions as the Bay Area Writing Project, the Lilly Endowment, and the National Council of Teachers of English; he has consulted on test development with the Educational Testing Service, the National Assessment of Educational Progress, the Association of American Medical Colleges, and many universities, community colleges, and school districts. As a member of the executive committee of the Council of Writing Program Administrators, he has participated in writing program evaluations of a wide variety of postsecondary institutions. His articles on measurement, teaching, writing, and literature have appeared in many journals, including *College English, College Composition and Communication, Journal of Basic Studies, College Board Review, Studies in English Literature, Review of English Studies,* and *Nineteenth Century Fiction.* His series of monographs describing the English Equivalency Examination (*Comparison and Contrast,* 1973–1981) is available through ERIC.

White was principal investigator for Research in Effective Teaching of Writing, a project funded by the National Institute of Education, 1980–1985. Initial reports on the project have been published in *WPA,* the journal of the Council of Writing Program Administrators; and a two-volume final report is available through ERIC (White and Polin, 1986). His most recent book, *Teaching and Assessing Writing* (1985), was widely reviewed and has been called "required reading for the profession."

Developing Successful
College Writing Programs

Chapter 1

Improving the Campus Climate for Writing Programs

For most faculty and administrators, the importance of writing is axiomatic, rather like the need for higher salaries or more parking space. Writing is a Good Thing, and no more justification is usually required. It is also generally agreed that students should write better than they do. From time to time someone, often in the English department, comes up with a program or a grant to improve student writing, and the institution devotes considerable attention and resources to the new plan. The older faculty remark, more in sorrow than in cynicism, that they have seen that innovation before and that little seems to change over the years. Texts, syllabuses, even faculty may be changed, but the students still seem to write the way they did before. The Good Thing just doesn't get better.

But when we look at different campuses, we notice that "writing" (however it is defined—the definitions shift about a great deal) seems to matter more and happen more successfully on some campuses than on others. Evidence from several recent studies supports the personal experience of every visiting professor: the "campus climate for writing" is as real as the New England snow or the Oregon rain (White and Polin, 1986). Unlike the weather, however, the campus climate for writing can be changed. While changes in one aspect of the program may bring about partial or temporary improvements, research suggests that

1

small changes are not nearly as effective as alterations in the entire writing program. The most effective way to improve student writing on a campus, therefore, is to understand the conditions that produce the campus climate for writing and to improve them systematically.

Cognitive Versus Reductionist Definitions of Writing

Each generation of writers and teachers has recognized the value of writing or rhetoric as part of thinking and learning. In the beginning, as John tells us, was the Word, and the power of the word has always been obvious. The best teachers in all fields have traditionally required writing and revision as a pathway to, as well as evidence of, understanding. Just as traditionally, the tendency to reduce education to mechanical and functional training has always been present. Our day is no exception.

In the 1980s, the importance of writing has been reasserted by a series of well-publicized reports by governmental agencies, private foundations, and educational organizations assessing American education. One of these reports, by a committee of the Association of American Colleges (1985), points with considerable alarm at "widespread public skepticism about the quality of higher education" and the "loss of integrity in the bachelor's degree" (p. 18). Typically, the report includes a set of recommendations for the baccalaureate curriculum, emphasizing what college graduates may be expected to know. The first two (of nine) major recommendations to the university community happen to focus on what is (or should be) central to writing programs (pp. 18–19):

> 1. *Inquiry, abstract logical thinking, critical analysis.* How do we know? Why do we believe? What is the evidence? Here, whatever the subject matter, we are at the heart of the intellectual process, concerned with the phenomenon of human thinking, the processes whereby [we] establish a fact, put two or more of them together, come to conclusions as to their meaning, and perhaps even

soar with some leap of imagination to a thought that has never been thought before. To reason well, to recognize when reason and evidence are not enough, to discover the legitimacy of intuition, to subject inert data to the probing analysis of the mind—these are the primary experiences required of the undergraduate course of study. There is not a subject taught nor a discipline entrenched in the curriculum that should fail to provide students with a continuing practice in thinking of the kind we here discuss. Probably most of us, inside and outside the academic community, assume that if anything is paid attention to in our colleges and universities, thinking must be it. Unfortunately, thinking can be lazy. It can be sloppy. It can be reactive rather than active. It can be inert. It can be fooled, misled, bullied. In colleges and universities it is all of these things, as well as perceptive, deep, imaginative, careful, quick, and clever. Students possess great untrained and untapped capacities for logical thinking, critical analysis, and inquiry, but these are capacities that are not spontaneous; they grow out of wise instruction, experience, encouragement, correction, and constant use.

2. *Literacy: writing, reading, speaking, listening.* Literacy is a heavy word, a concept so full of meaning that it is often misused to mean more and less than it does. For us, writing, as literacy, means being in possession of language, knowing its shapes and possibilities, being so accustomed to its grammar and rules that the why is unnecessary, always aware that writing is an expression of thinking, a give-away of how we think and feel and judge. Writing can be effusive, stiff, controlled, explosive; it is always revealing of what lies behind it. Since a baccalaureate education is intended to lead young men and women to a satisfying possession of themselves, then writing should lead them there.

Clarity, directness, simplicity even in the ordering of complicated ideas, originality, and playful fun in the use of words—these are some of the goals that should guide students in their experience with writing as an exercise in literacy. . . .

Not every word or combination of words, whether read or written or spoken, can be expressions of unassailable style, models of taste and beauty that will endure. Some of us are better at these things than others, but none of us should be given up for lost. There are pleasures in sharing human excellence, even while trying and failing to be the best. A bachelor's degree should mean that its holders can read, write, and speak at levels of distinction and have been given many opportunities to learn how. It also should mean that many of them do so with style.

Although the AAC committee statement (which is echoed in most of the other reports on this topic) takes aim at the college baccalaureate curriculum as a whole, it is particularly appropriate as a starting point for consideration of the role of writing, and the writing program, on campus. It asserts that writing can be learned and should be taught; it defines writing as an active means of thought and learning, a way to discover what one means and who one is. Such a definition, which I share, is itself a powerful argument for the importance of writing as a central part of the undergraduate degree. The definition moves beyond a merely functional or mechanical view of writing and beyond a merely departmental view of writing instruction.

But it would be naive to imagine that many, or even most, campuses in America define writing in this way. Many faculty and administrators regard writing as a passive act, a mere communication of what is known or read. On many, or even most, campuses, writing is a narrow concern of the English department, which is then a handy scapegoat to be blamed for the errors in punctuation, spelling, and syntax that undergraduates routinely commit. This reductionist definition leads to a writing program designed as "therapy," to use Albert Kitzhaber's term (1963)—a basically "remedial" enterprise aimed at the improvement of spelling and sentence structure. Such a mechanical program is usually deemed unworthy of the full-time faculty, even if it is grudgingly awarded baccalaureate credit. It becomes an unwelcome burden placed on the English department, which usually in turn deposits it ungraciously on graduate students, part-timers, and lecturers. Frequently, such necessities as a private office for student conferences, secretarial support, and access to the duplicating machines are not available for these composition faculty. In a natural choice, these fringe faculty try to escape this "demeaning labor"; meanwhile, they do the best they can to teach under difficult circumstances. Sometimes an unspoken romantic rhetoric of exclusion lies behind these attitudes. That is, the tenured literature faculty may believe that writing ability is an innate talent that only the select few possess; those without the gift, by this elitist logic, can never learn to write, and it is a waste of professorial time to try to teach them. (See Russell, 1988, for a history of this view of composition instruction.) Although the romantic view of writing might seem to be the opposite of the utilitarian one, in practice they both lead to a general depreciation of the meaning and value of writing instruction.

Clearly, writing must be both creative and functional, both a cognitive process and a presented product for evaluation or action; and in most writing courses, teachers will naturally devote some attention to all aspects of the writing process, from conception through editing. Part of the problem of teaching writing is that it makes many different kinds of demands on both teachers and students. We want imaginative ideas, not imaginative spelling; we want individual reading, interpretation, and thinking, but we also insist on conformist punctuation and sentence structure. In the same way, we want all faculty to use writing as part of learning, but we want the English department to house much of the direct teaching, particularly for the ill prepared. Despite these conflicting demands, the claims for writing as a part of the baccalaureate curriculum do not rest on its mechanics, or on the undoubted value of writing as preparation for various jobs or careers, or even on its power for communicating what is already known. Writing is important, even central, to liberal education because writing stimulates (even as it records) the processes of learning, thinking, discovering, combining, evaluating, and imagining.

Despite their unfortunate recent history as reluctant custodians of writing instruction, English departments—with their built-in professional concern for careful reading and sensitive use of language—remain the appropriate home for writing courses and for university leadership of writing programs. But writing programs are too important and too wide ranging to be left for merely departmental planning; furthermore, too many English departments still assign writing a low priority among their competing enterprises. Writing in contemporary culture is an enabling discipline that makes education active and participatory; it is indispensable for the development of thought. Therefore, writing cannot remain just one more concern of the department in which it is housed; writing programs require the special attention of those responsible for the entire undergraduate curriculum.

Components and Features of Effective Writing Programs

Two research projects, one in California and the other in Texas, have recently been funded by federal agencies (the National Institute of Education and the Fund for the Improvement of Post-Secondary Education) to look closely at the effectiveness of college-level writing programs. Both of them began with definitions, a more complex task than either had anticipated. The California project developed a lozenge-shaped diagram, showing the interplay among the four components in a "Taxonomy of Writing Program Features": administrative structure (at the top of the diagram), composition faculty and the composition program (on the next level, at opposite sides of the diagram), and students (at the bottom of the diagram). The California study cautions against isolating the instructional "program" from its institutional context: "[This figure,] with its lines of force indicating movement in both directions, shows the actual form and operation of a composition program as the result of a complex set of relations among faculty, administrators, and students. The program cannot be described as an abstraction apart from the individuals who give it life." The study does see "an identifiable structure" behind most writing programs, as a result of the campus context, but notes that both "circumstances" and "individual decisions" keep changing that structure (White and Polin, 1986, vol. 1, p. 66).

The Texas study presents an even more elaborate conception of writing programs, portraying them as a series of concentric circles representing five levels: (1) the cultural and social context, (2) the institutional context, (3) the program structure and administration, (4) the content or curriculum, and (5) instruction. The surveys of the Texas team show (as do the surveys and interviews of the California team) that writing program directors have widely varying concepts of the meaning of their programs: "That relatively few directors cited any one successful aspect of college writing programs suggests that those programs vary considerably from one institutional context to another, from one department to another, from one director to another. . . . We also found considerable evidence of a variety of approaches to writing program administration, with some directors investing considerable energy in one area while others focus on another area" (Witte and others, 1981, pp. 103–104).

Each of these research studies isolates a series of program features, within the larger program context, which have the advantage of being limited and changeable. In general, we can state that a well-developed writing program contains the following features:

1. Preenrollment testing, counseling, and placement of students.
2. Coursework and support services for students who place at various levels on these tests.
3. Agreed-upon and applied criteria for student writing performance at the various levels of coursework.
4. Faculty training and retraining programs, including writing-

across-the-curriculum programs (that is, writing instruction outside the English department) to reinforce the uses of writing in learning all subjects.

5. A faculty assignment and reward structure that takes into account the special demands on writing teachers.
6. Advanced writing courses and support services for students beyond the freshman year and outside the English major.
7. General education requirements at the upper-division level embodying a sophisticated definition of writing.
8. An assessment design (perhaps part of institutional self-study) calling for periodic review of the writing program.

The California project found that program features reflect a campus attitude toward writing. That is, behind the components of an effective writing program stand an interested and informed administration providing resources and incentives, an effective English department providing skills and leadership, a concerned faculty willing to consider ways to increase the active learning of their students, and students aware that writing is important outside of the freshman English class. When these campus characteristics are present, a full writing program can be developed without too many difficulties; academic leadership will find ways to mobilize existing attitudes (and curricula) and express those attitudes in an overall plan.

But when those attitudes are not present—or (more likely) are minority sentiments overwhelmed by many competing claims on student, faculty, and administrative attention—academic leadership is put to the test. If the English department will not provide skills and leadership in writing (a crucial need), how is such leadership to be found and nurtured? If the faculty feel that writing is none of their business, or that writing is just one more discipline competing for resources and turf, how are such faculty to be "developed"? If the learning center is dominated by machines, or starved for resources or room or personnel, or if it is too involved with every department's individual needs to pay attention to writing, where are students to go for help? If the campus culture is focused on technology or professional careers or sports, how are students to believe that writing matters? Under such circumstances, not everything can be done at once. The campus must start somewhere, and the natural place to begin is the English department.

Role of English Departments in Establishing the Campus Climate for Writing

Recent research confirms the commonsense view that a campus English department is the focus for concern (if there is to be concern) about writing. The English department need not take responsibility away from the campus as a whole or from the students themselves; but it must provide the leadership and the professional knowledge for campus writing programs if the campus climate for writing is to be a positive one.

We must be cautious when we generalize about English departments in relation to writing instruction, since the campus situation is likely to differ from one kind of institution to another. We need not fret about a lack of concern for writing in community college English departments; for them, writing courses are not only the bread and butter but most of the rest of the meal as well. The English departments of highly selective research universities, on the other hand, are likely to rely almost entirely on their (usually untrained) graduate students to teach writing, while the tenured faculty spend their time teaching literature courses and writing about literature. The great majority of institutions in America lie between these extremes, with their English departments uncertain about the priority to assign to writing instruction within and outside the department. The tendency of these institutions to look to the major research universities for their models poses severe problems; their less elite student bodies particularly need writing programs, while their models for departmental structure and priorities consider such programs as unwanted or undesirable stepchildren.

However, even the major research universities manifest sporadic concern about the writing abilities of their elite undergraduate student bodies, and occasional guilt that the Ph.D.s and ABDs they place on the job market have received very little training in the teaching of writing. And, as a recent survey by the Modern Language Association (MLA) suggests, such training may now be available for some doctorate candidates in English: 31 percent of the Ph.D. programs participating in this survey indicated that programs or options in writing either exist or are planned (Denham, 1987). Another recent survey found that 53 out of 123 doctoral programs "claimed to offer a specialization in composition and rhetoric" (Chapman and Tate, 1987, p. 125).

Nonetheless, until very recently, despite increasing pressures from writing researchers and the academic community at large, very few English Ph.D. programs have given more than passing attention to the teaching of writing (Chapman and Tate, 1987). Most new faculty, even today, have taught freshman composition as graduate assistants, but few of them have been in a genuine writing program that provided more than a nodding acquaintance with writing research or pedagogy.

Unhappily, the new English faculty member, fresh from graduate school, may even have absorbed the distaste or even contempt for writing instruction that prevails in many well-reputed English departments. Skeptical of the advances in the field over the last two decades, and sometimes unaware of the rhetorical roots of their own discipline, many senior professors regard the teaching of composition as apprentice work for young scholars while they are writing on serious topics, such as literary theory or Shakespeare's metaphors. When one gains tenure, it is time to put away childish things, such as the teaching of writing, and get about what many of these senior faculty take to be the real work of the English department: the training of future literature professors and the publication of literary or critical scholarship. This attitude surfaces like unconscious racism even from those traditionalists whose best friends are writing teachers and who are truly concerned about writing. One distinguished emeritus professor, for instance, writing about the use of computers in the teaching of freshmen, speaks in passing of the difficult labors of "those sentenced to teach the nation's composition courses" (Kern, 1987). The metaphor is clear, despite the overt and demonstrated interest in composition: after serving the sentence, assuming time off for good behavior, the teacher can be released into a better world, where composition need not be endured.

Thus, the newly minted regular English Ph.D. with real training in and respect for the teaching of writing (such a creature does exist; I have seen several in their native habitat) is a rare bird who has shown diligence, tenacity, and responsibility beyond the average. He, or more likely she, may well be self-taught, or the acolyte of a self-taught tenured maverick on the graduate faculty. Until very recently, however, anyone who expressed a scholarly interest in writing instruction elicited murmurs from some senior mentors, who raised dark questions about that person's seriousness and future. And, despite the signs of new programs, special Ph.D.s in rhetoric and composition will be in short supply for many years. In 1985–86, a total of only twenty institutions granted 228 such degrees; 102 of them were from three universities: Southern California, Indiana of Pennsylvania, and Pittsburgh (Chapman and Tate, 1987, p. 128).

The Writing Program Administrator

Since the balance of power and disciplinary respect in most English departments is usually tilted against the teaching of writing, except as income generation, writing specialists are not likely to be selected as department chairs. Thus, the crucial administrator for writing programs turns out to be a minor functionary with few prerogatives, little assigned time, and negligible status: the writing program administrator (WPA). I use here the WPA abbreviation, following the name of the journal started by the Council of Writing Program Administrators in 1980. Many campuses use less elaborate titles for this position: writing coordinator, director of composition, chair of the composition committee, or the like. Some campuses have no such position, leaving such duties as may be needed to the spare time of the English department chair.

In keeping with the low prestige that writing as a field continues to suffer in most English departments, many WPAs are appointed to the job by rotation, as if to say that the job is an unpleasant one that anyone can do. (Some English departments rotate chairs almost as casually, enfeebling departmental administration as well.) On some campuses, the principal qualification for the WPA is a genial personality and an interest in graduate students. On a few others, the job is treated quite cynically, particularly if it is accompanied by some released time from teaching; on these campuses, the job not only is rotated among the senior faculty who need extra time for their literary scholarship but is even split up among them. Thus, there may be a remedial writing coordinator, a freshman composition director, an upper-division writing committee chair, and a supervisor of placement testing—perhaps all of them literary scholars with the slimmest of training or interest in the teaching of writing. The California researchers found, however, that students write better on campuses where there is a single WPA for the writing program as a whole, as opposed to those campuses where separate administrators coordinate the remedial, the freshman, and the upper-division writing courses (White and Polin, 1986, vol. 1, p. 320).

As the first major step in improving the campus climate for writing, a WPA should be given overall responsibility for coordinating the campus writing program. While a few universities have made such a post a separate line, reporting directly to the central administration, this radical departure from current practice seems unable to maintain itself for long. Probably the most successful place for this administrator remains the English department, where a natural (if fragmentary) constituency resides. But more important than the location of this person are the status, qualifications, and support for the job.

There are many ways to enhance the WPA's status. In the first place, the job should be comprehensive, dealing with all aspects of the writing program. Second, the position should be given to a serious and trained professional. The WPA should be an experienced teacher of writing; a published author and editor of articles, books, and texts on writing; a member of such professional organizations as the Conference on College Composition and Communication; a senior professor with sufficient standing in the campus community to command attention for the writing program. Third, the responsibilities for the position should be carefully spelled out. The WPA should be given substantial responsibility for appointing and evaluating writing teachers; developing policies, curricula, and procedures; training and retraining faculty, both within and outside the English department; making decisions about placement, equivalency, and exit tests; and teaching courses in such specialties as rhetoric or writing research, as well as writing classes. Furthermore, the WPA should be the acknowledged spokesperson for the writing program, both on and off the campus, and should receive enough assigned time and clerical support so that he or she can carry out the functions of the job.

When a campus has this kind of WPA, the effects are far reaching. The California project posits this kind of leadership as the underlying variable behind the data it produced on a wide variety of issues. For example, that project found a series of significant correlations between the strength of campus leadership for graduation requirements in writing and the performance of the weakest writers in freshman composition courses. It found a similar correlation between faculty development programs and the performance of these same low-ability students at the freshman level. Although these significant correlations probably do not express direct cause-and-effect relationships, a strong WPA may well be the underlying common cause—a sign that composition matters to the campus.

Role of Campus Administration in Improving Campus Climate for Writing

The campus administration needs to recognize that writing is not the sole property or sole responsibility of the English department. Even though the leadership of that department is necessary if much action is to occur, a great many other resources are in fact devoted to aspects of writing. The dean of students will report that much time in the counseling center is spent on writing problems and that a major portion of the budget for the special admissions program (or the educational opportunity program, or whatever the support program for underrepresented student groups may be called) is going for writing tutors. The testing office is likely to be heavily involved in placement testing for entering students, equivalency testing for high-ability students challenging writing courses, or exit-level testing for the baccalaureate degree. The learning center may be torn between an inexhaustible (and exhausting) demand for writing tutors and all the other needs of students.

Meanwhile, community business leaders may be complaining about the writing ability of the university graduates they employ, and the high schools may be asking for help as their students encounter writing proficiency requirements for diplomas. Students enrolled in teacher training programs are facing writing examinations before receiving teaching credentials, and they are looking for help from an unresponsive curriculum; they also expect to teach writing throughout their careers, and they have received only scattered training in how to do it from their English education courses. The English department is reluctant to add more writing courses, since there are already insufficient literature courses for the English majors and there are only so many faculty; many English departments are deeply concerned that their important role as teachers and scholars of literature will disappear as they respond to an almost insatiable demand for writing instruction.

There are, of course, many ways for an effective administration to focus attention, resources, and personnel to deal with these familiar problems. As I have said, the appointment of an appropriate WPA is probably the first step. The appointment of a committee to develop an effective, instruction-based upper-division writing requirement ought perhaps to be the second step. The important advantage of writing tests at various levels, for various purposes, should be obtained. Some integration of writing support services and writing courses should be attempted; perhaps mere communication between those involved will be a revolutionary beginning. And a writing-across-the-curriculum program ought to receive high priority; such a program not only adds to the supply of faculty informed about writing but relieves the concern of the English department that it alone will be asked to carry full responsibility.

All these activities, and more, will be necessary if the campus climate for writing is to be improved. None of them is easy to accomplish, since campus traditions and departmental patterns have normally scattered responsibility for writing. On most campuses, there is a certain unanimity of opinion on that score; whoever may be speaking tends to be sure that someone else is responsible for the improvement of student writing, which, of course, badly needs improvement. When all members of the campus community, particularly the administration and the faculty outside the English department, begin accepting their share of this responsibility, the campus climate will probably begin to improve and the education of students will certainly improve. There is plenty of responsibility to go around, plenty of blame for us all, and plenty of work to be done. The rest of this book seeks to move systematically through the various issues involved in this effort.

Chapter 2

Insights from Research
on Existing Programs

It is not easy to discover what is going on, or why, in any college writing program. The research describing these programs is surprisingly constricted. Although a few studies do yield important information, most prove to be elaborate show-and-tell exercises. They list the successes and (rarely) failures of specific teaching ideas but usually do not permit generalizations or replication outside of their originating environments. Special studies of individual teachers and the learning of individual students are readily available (Emig, 1971; Elbow, 1973; Berkenkotter and Murray, 1983), as are descriptions of sample programs (Maimon, 1981; Connolly and Vilardi, 1986; Hartzog, 1986); but if we want to discover how writing can be taught and learned on our own campus, we must be able to generalize reliably.

When we try to generalize about the teaching of writing in college, we need to look closely at writing programs, though we should be aware that some teachers will persist in doing as much as possible in their own way, no matter what the program may direct. That is, composition teachers usually see themselves as independent operators doing the best they can with their classes, and they tend to be skeptical or resistant if someone offers unwanted advice about composition teaching. But the illusion of independence extends only to certain aspects of the curriculum and to the interactions that take place between student and teacher. Composition teaching is necessarily constrained in many ways by the writing program and the external setting. The types and numbers of students in the class, the goals of the instruction, the kinds of texts and assignments, the standards for grading—all these and more are usually established by forces outside the instructor's control. In many cases, the writing program also determines the kind of teaching that takes place.

The six reports described here are general in scope and provide some insight into the issues and important factors to consider in examining any program of writing instruction. These studies have sought to describe the national scene in college English, most often through national survey data and selective interviews. One additional report (Hillocks, 1986), to be dealt with in the next chapter, describes research in composition instruction; while not directly concerned with writing programs, this research has important implications for them. Only two of these reports—the California study (White and Polin, 1986) and the Hillocks study—attempted to evaluate the success of program features in helping faculty to teach better or students to write better; neither study is particularly convincing in its findings in this area, Thus, there are few data-based recommendations that can help composition directors, composition committees, department chairs, college administrators, and instructors make decisions among a range of options whose success may be closely linked to particular settings or policies or personnel. But we can review the goals and classroom activities reported during the last twenty-five years and notice a certain consistency in them.

Six Research Studies: What Goes On in Writing Programs?

The Kitzhaber Study. One of the earliest systematic studies of college composition programs was published in 1963. Albert Kitzhaber's report on college composition begins with a discussion of the contradictory goals or purposes that then (as well as now) lay behind the curriculum and instruction in college writing courses. Kitzhaber describes "therapy" programs as those designed to remedy the ill-prepared entering freshman student, thus providing a "service" to the students and for the faculty in other departments by teaching these students to write with "reasonable ease, precision, and correctness" (p. 2). Other programs are concerned with cognitive development rather than correctness; that is, they are designed "to focus the student's attention on fundamental principles of clear thinking and the clear and effective written expression of that thinking, and to give him disciplined practice in the principles" (p. 3).

These two perspectives on composition programs, with their different if not necessarily competing goals, suggest differences in locating the responsibility for teaching students to be competent college writers. Where writing instruction is performed as a service, primary responsibility for the success of this service is normally left to the English department. Where writing instruction is part of the general intellectual training received in college, other departments share the responsibility; they should "foster the same discipline but direct it toward the varying demands of the specific subject matters" (pp. 3–4).

In addition to these contrasting views, different English department specialties—such as semantics, logic, classical rhetoric, linguistics, literature, or literary criticism—may guide a writing program, depending on the particular expertness of the department chair or the composition director. But there is no "proof," Kitzhaber points out, that instructional activities derived from any of these particular specialties bring about gains in student achievement. The difficulties arise because prospective researchers cannot identify or control effects resulting from students' past experiences and effects from the particular personality traits and teaching competencies of instructors. Furthermore, the various measures of student gains may not be sufficiently sensitive or valid. In short, Kitzhaber pointed out the many problems to be discovered by empirical program evaluators in the succeeding generation—namely, that programs, students, teachers, and writing itself are all too complex for conventional educational research methods.

After discussing these problems, Kitzhaber reports the results of his own data-gathering effort, the purpose of which was to describe the variety in writing programs offered in American four-year universities. Kitzhaber collected syllabuses from ninety-five universities and analyzed the descriptions of writing courses—specifically, the expressed goals, content, progression in instructional content, and texts. Interested in the veracity of these syllabuses, he paid follow-up visits to eighteen of the campuses to determine the extent to which courses were implemented as described.

This portion of the Kitzhaber study led to four findings: (1) There was great variety in approaches to writing instruction. (2) A similar variety in composition texts (as opposed to substantial agreement for other college courses) suggested a lack of rigor and scholarship. (3) Writing program structures seemed to express doubts about the competence of writing instructors. (4) Larger institutions depended on part-time instructors or lecturers to a greater extent than did smaller institutions.

When Kitzhaber tried to evaluate the Dartmouth composition program, he ran into problems of measurement that he could not surmount. The evaluation method he chose, an elaborate count of errors in student-written drafts, did not take into account the increasing quality or complexity of the writing tasks given to students as they move through college. (The research design problems he encountered have continued to bedevil program evaluators to this day, as the last chapter of this book will show.) He found that seniors committed more writing errors than freshmen did and concluded that this showed a decline in writing skill during the college years. His "demonstration" that Dartmouth seniors write less well than freshmen serves as a warning to evaluators that more sophisticated and more complex measurement devices than error counts are required if results are to be credible.

Kitzhaber's work is valuable less for its evaluations or descriptive information, which may no longer be valid (although most later researchers discovered many of the same patterns that he did), than for its identification of key concepts and definitions that ought to be considered in the investigation of college writing programs. Clearly, campus size and the philosophy or goals of the composition program are important factors in determining what takes place in classrooms and who is doing the teaching. He also suggests attention to the following: training of the staff, texts, amount of writing assigned, where writing is done (in class or out), and the direction, structure, and guidance given to students.

The Wilcox Survey. A decade later, Thomas Wilcox conducted the National Survey of Undergraduate Programs in English, sponsored by the National Council of Teachers of English and funded by the (then) United States Office of Education. Like Kitzhaber, Wilcox (1973) collected survey data (questionnaires from English department chairs) and interview data. His survey data describe the makeup of department staffs in terms of status categories and the reward systems in effect. Large universities, he found, preferred to hire specialists in literary fields, distinguished scholars in particular, and overused cheap labor—in the form of part-time and non-tenure-track appointments and graduate assistants—for writing instruction. Small colleges, in contrast, preferred to hire generalists, emphasized effective teaching rather than publishing, and tended toward "top-heaviness" characterized by a predominantly stable, tenured staff isolated from "new ideas and enthusiasms" presumably generated by newer and younger staff members.

In contrast to Kitzhaber, who concentrated on course content and instruction in composition, Wilcox concentrated his reporting on the administrative properties of English departments: department autonomy, teacher evaluation, staffing, and philosophies underlying composition and remedial courses. He assumed that these characteristics and decisions also affect the nature of instruction. Like Kitzhaber, Wilcox recognizes a relationship between campus size and staffing patterns, and between philosophies about writing instruction and the organization and content of writing courses. The new information in the Wilcox study concerns the evaluation of instructors and the organization of writing courses.

In describing information on teacher evaluation, Wilcox raises two issues: desired characteristics and their measurement. His survey data suggest some degree of consensus about the characteristics that evaluators seek in instructors. The two descriptions receiving endorsement by more than 75 percent of the Wilcox sample are (1) "stimulation and motivation" and (2) "knowledge and mastery of subject matter." The next three top selections are (3) "enthusiasm and interest" (40 percent), (4) "rapport with students" (39 percent), and (5) "fresh ideas and critical insights" (35 percent). Interestingly, the five most valued teacher traits suggest a greater concern for the general characteristics of good teachers than for specialized competence or particular knowledge or approach in composition.

Wilcox next asked the department administrators in his study how they determined whether an instructor had these characteristics. Here he describes the basic problem of "how to obtain reliable and accurate evidence of what actually occurs in each instructor's classroom" (p. 29). The most common source of information cited by the survey respondents was informal personal contacts with the instructors (93 percent). The second most common answer was the review of assignments, exams, and other teaching materials (51 percent). Curiously, for 1973, student evaluations of instructors (evaluations solicited by the department or the administration) were cited by only 40 percent of the respondents and class observations by only 36 percent. Other sources of information included informal contacts with students, student-published evaluations of staff, solicited colleague opinions, comparisons of how well the teacher's students perform on common examinations, and the instructor's performance in department meetings.

Wilcox also asked his survey population whether all instructors covered the course content in a generally uniform way and how this uniformity (or course consistency) was achieved. His findings suggest that absolute consistency is not normally regarded as desirable (since it can interfere with an individual teacher's style), although most respondents "believe that all legitimate means to achieve uniformity should be tried" (p. 48). Among the choices for methods of establishing course consistency are the following: staff meetings (68 percent), use of syllabuses (62 percent), common texts selected by committee (62 percent), and, less popularly, common exams (22 percent), common lectures (12 percent), and common theme grading (1.2 percent). For Wilcox, these findings lead to the unanswered question of "whether there can be—or ought to be—a right way to teach college English" (p. 49).

When he focuses on composition, Wilcox—like Kitzhaber ten years earlier—found that "English departments in the United States are about evenly divided between those that offer the freshman utilitarian training and those that offer him something more" (p. 79). But, instead of distinguishing between " 'therapy' and a course in 'clear thinking,' " many departments "see theirs as a choice . . . between exercising and educating, between coaching students for future occasions which may demand the use of language and confronting them with present occasions which require the use of all their mental faculties" (p. 79).

Wilcox is particularly critical of the content of courses in remedial English. The typical course, he found, "usually consists of little more than elementary drill in the mechanics of language," with textbooks "of the kind used in some junior high schools" and short—often single-paragraph—papers assigned. "There can be little intellectual substance in these courses, which the students aptly call 'bonehead English' " (p. 68).

The Austin Research Project. Although the Kitzhaber study and the Wilcox study are landmarks in their sparse field of inquiry, they predate what Richard Young (1978) and Maxine Hairston (1982) have called the "paradigm shift" occasioned by the intense interest in and instructional research about the writing process. This view of composition posits a traditional paradigm, based on correctness and an emphasis on the writing product, now being replaced by a more informed paradigm of instruction based on critical thinking and an emphasis on the writing process. This paradigmatic view of composition has been disputed by Robert Connors (1983) and C. H. Knoblauch (1985) and redefined by Steven North as an "inter-methodological struggle for power" (1987, pp. 318–321). North admits that "there has unquestionably been a shift in the internal order of the Society of Composition" (p. 320). Thus, one might suppose that the information provided by the early studies of writing programs is out of date and only of historical interest. However, similar work with similar findings was recently completed at the University of Texas at Austin, supported by the Fund for the Improvement of Post-Secondary Education (Witte and others, 1981).

The Austin research team was primarily interested in developing guidelines and methods for colleges to use in evaluating composition programs (Witte and Faigley, 1983). As a preliminary activity, they conducted a national survey of college composition program administrators. This national profile includes and distinguishes results from two- and four-year colleges as well as public and private universities. Witte and his colleagues have reported the range of practices in (1) writing course content and sequence, (2) staffing of writing courses, (3) textbooks and other teaching materials, (4) instructional activities, (5) student evaluation and proficiency testing, and (6) faculty evaluation and development. Again, as in the Kitzhaber and Wilcox studies, institutional size seemed to be a clear factor in distinguishing among actual practices in these six areas, particularly in the use of part-timers, lecturers, and teaching assistants.

The update of instructional information by the Austin team is remarkably unremarkable in the light of the major changes that have occurred in composition theory and in research-based recommendations for instructional activities since the 1960s (Cooper and Odell, 1978; White, 1985; Hillocks, 1986). The Austin data describe the continued popularity of grammar and rhetoric texts in beginning composition in both two-year and four-year colleges and universities; the only real distinction is that universities also report greater use of nonfiction anthologies.

The new information on staffing is perhaps more interesting because of the care with which the Austin team has distinguished among faculty status categories. As a result of their care, we now have data to support the current, otherwise unsupported, belief that differences in writing instruction may be traceable to differences in staff status. For example, the data reveal disparities in faculty development opportunities for full-time, tenured faculty and non-tenure-track faculty. These disparities are in part related to the size of the institution, most likely because the larger institutions employ a greater number of part-time, non-tenure-track instructors. The universities seem to be providing the most training in composition for all categories of staffing, though slightly more energy is directed toward the part-timers. Two-year colleges, on the other hand, aim most of their workshop activity toward the tenured and tenure-track full-timers.

Another particularly relevant aspect of the Austin survey data is the self-report by composition program directors on the successes of their programs. Several program components were repeatedly listed as "successful" by the questionnaire respondents: (1) the independent writing lab, (2) teacher training efforts, (3) peer tutoring and other collaborative learning, and (4) placement procedures. The respondents also listed (without supporting evidence) a consistent set of "successful outcomes" for their programs, including (1) teaching students to write clear, effective prose for different audiences, (2) getting teachers to teach writing as a process, and (3) involving tenured faculty in teaching writing. Of the seven successful outcomes most often cited, four relate to program policy and organization. Clearly, these program-level decisions can have impact on instructional success; just as clearly, program outcomes encompass more than student gains.

The California Project. A five-year research study of the effectiveness of writing programs at the California State University (CSU) was completed in 1986. This huge system is composed of nineteen campuses enrolling approximately a third of a million students. Using an elaborate combination of surveys, interviews, outcome measures of several writing skills and attitudes, and computer data analysis, the research team produced a two-volume report entitled *Research in Effective Teaching of Writing* (White and Polin, 1986).

The following chapter will detail some of the findings in this report, particularly the results of the factor analysis of instructor-reported approaches to the teaching of writing. The researchers sent a twelve-page questionnaire to all full- and part-time faculty who were then teaching (or who regularly taught) either freshman or remedial writing classes on any of the nineteen CSU campuses during the spring of 1982. As a result of persistence, personal follow-up, and departmental support, the project was able to realize a very high return rate for the questionnaire: 56 percent, for a total of 418 respondents. The sample of instructors who returned the questionnaire included representative portions (for the CSU) of tenured, tenure-track, and part-time faculty, as well as a reasonable diversity of age groups and teaching specialties. About 60 percent of the sample reported completion of the Ph.D., and only 8.3 percent had less than an M.A.; a mere 5.4 percent of the respondents were graduate teaching assistants; a surprisingly high 14.7 percent were trained in fields outside English.

The sample of the study is particularly valuable for its representativeness across large and small campuses, for its high rate of return from all those teaching writing, and for the wealth of detail it provides. The sample cannot, of course, fully represent all college teaching in American higher education. It has a higher proportion of experienced faculty with doctorates teaching composition than will be the case in predominantly research universities, where almost all composition teaching is done by graduate students; concomitantly, community colleges will normally have a lower percentage of faculty with doctorates teaching composition, though a larger percentage of their English departments (often virtually everyone) is engaged in that teaching. Nonetheless, the sample does represent the spread of faculty who teach writing at the college level, and the detailed nature of the questionnaire provides more information about what goes on in writing classes than previous research could supply.

One of the most interesting findings of this study is that composition faculty tend to teach writing in much the same way, no matter what level of student or class they face. The research team had expected that instructional approach would differ from remedial to regular instruction, but they found that "our sample yields no such course-related differences in practices, methods, and goals" (vol. 2, p. 17). This "at first startling" lack of distinction between courses at different skill levels, according to the study, occurs because instructors have developed specific patterns of teaching writing, which they then seem to apply to all writing courses they teach:

Perhaps an instructor embraces a general set of methods and goals in regard to writing instruction generally and varies the level of difficulty or sophistication of specific class tasks and content to suit the student group. That is, the instructor perceives the change in level to be no more radical than the customary variation in ability among different class sections of the same course. This interpretation suggests that particular theories we hold about teaching writing operate as stable guidelines affecting changeable classroom practices. Thus, differences in any one instructor's remedial and regular composition instruction may not be as accurately measured by questions about theories of writing as by pace, content, grading criteria, and other day-to-day elements of teaching that express instructional theory. Results of data analyses show more instructional variety within the ranks of freshman composition than between freshman composition and remedial or other lower-division courses [White and Polin, 1986, vol. 2, pp. 17–18].

This finding suggests that the best route to discovering what is happening in composition classes is to find out what individual instructors do, rather than what program administrators think they are doing or want them to do. A different part of the questionnaire helped explain this interesting relationship between department policies and individual theories about the teaching of writing. The respondents were asked to rate various statements on a scale from "very important" to "not important at all." The statements provided a good range of perspectives, from "expose students to good literature" and "allow for practice in writing activities necessary for success in other college courses," to "teach invention skills, such as planning, prewriting, clustering, heuristics" and "allow for in-class writing in a workshop setting." Many faculty rated more than one instructional theme as "very important." They then were asked to indicate the source or reason for their ratings: department policy,

informal faculty agreement, course tradition, personal prefer-
ence, experimenting with new ideas, and "not applicable." Once
again, the results surprised the researchers:

> Unexpectedly, items on the source or reason for in-
> structional decisions did not show much variation
> of any sort (among faculty status, from campus to
> campus, or among course referents [level of instruc-
> tion]). For the most part, faculty consistently
> checked department policy *and* personal prefer-
> ence as the reasons behind their instructional prac-
> tices, a curious combination in the light of the vari-
> ety of practices normally used by so many faculty
> in the same department.
>
> The most likely reason for this combination,
> in our judgment, is that many department policies
> may be general enough to be all things to all peo-
> ple; in such a case, there is a policy supporting
> every teacher's practices, whatever those practices
> may be. Some faculty may have checked "depart-
> ment policy" as an influence even when there is no
> policy at all, since no policy suggests general ap-
> proval of whatever may occur. We suspect that the
> faculty and the department in most cases give so
> little attention to alternatives for classroom prac-
> tice that most composition teachers simply imagine
> that what they do is department policy; it thus be-
> comes possible to be an autonomous teacher who
> conforms to department rules no matter what one
> does [vol. 2, p. 14].

While these survey data suggest that we need to be skeptical about program descriptions and goals supplied by administrators, the researchers did find important program differences
in both their survey and outcome data. Many of those differences seemed to be related to campus policies and environment
rather than to departmental philosophies or practices. Nonetheless, the WPA certainly has, or can have, a profound influence

on many aspects of the program. One of these influences emerged when the researchers attempted to discover differences between the way that tenured or tenure-track faculty and lecturers or part-timers teach writing. The two ways in which the part-time faculty differed from their more secure colleagues tended to show the stronger departmental influence on them, rather than a clear quality difference.

Of the six instructional modes defined by the factor analysis (the next chapter will look at them in detail), the tenured or tenure-track faculty as a group differed from lecturers or part-time teachers in their use of the "text-based rhetoric approach." This approach is generally rejected by the regular faculty ($p = .001$) and approved by the others ($p = .05$). This difference suggests that the part-time teachers tend to be more, not less, conservative in their classes than those on the tenure track. Or it may suggest that the temporary faculty, sometimes hired just before (sometimes even after) classes begin, are accustomed to teaching with conventional materials chosen for them by the WPA.

A second difference between the replies from temporary teachers as a group and the tenure/tenure-track group had to do with the much greater variety within the temporary group. Though individual teachers in the tenure group disagreed with one another, the patterns of responses of that group turned out to be much more similar across campuses than dissimilar. In contrast, the lecturers and part-timers showed different patterns of responses by campus. That is, the temporary faculty show preferences for one or another approach to composition "as a function of the campus on which the instructors teach, not the course they teach" (p. 298). The researchers explain this "odd finding" as a probable effect of the campus WPA's ideas on part-time faculty, who are "in no position to treat those ideas with the kind of skepticism typical of those more secure in their position" (p. 299).

The study also found that part-time faculty are likely to use three of the six approaches to composition teaching that will be discussed in the next chapter. The text-based rhetoric approach allows teachers hired at the last minute to make individual selections from an anthology chosen by others. The individualized writing lab and the service course approaches do not rely on textbooks at all, but on the interpersonal skills and common knowledge of library research that part-timers typically possess. Since part-timers on different campuses showed clear preferences for one or another of these approaches, the researchers concluded that the WPA was able to convince these teachers to use his or her favorite theory of composition instruction. Once again, the findings demonstrate that the WPA is likely to have far more influence over the temporary faculty than over the tenured and tenure-track staff (vol. 1, pp. 298–300).

The research was unable to make a connection between current classroom practice, reflecting various theories of composition, and its various outcome measures. It does show both the diversity of approaches and a way of systematically organizing and considering the value of those approaches, in the context of the entire campus writing program in action. Furthermore, the research suggests new approaches to writing and program assessment, to the roles of various program administrators, and to the relation of the writing program to the campus environment. Had the sample been more representative of the true role of the graduate assistant in American colleges (only 5.4 percent of the respondents were teaching assistants), it might have shown a much more dramatic effect on writing instruction by active WPAs.

The California study has added important information in many areas of composition instruction, and it will reappear in this book when its findings are appropriate to the topic under discussion. Its particular contribution to knowledge is largely a function of the resources that went into the research: a research team made up of experienced English faculty and WPAs, educational researchers, and computer specialists; the application of sophisticated research methodologies and computer data analysis; the use of very large samples; and a focus on detail.

Two 1986 MLA Publications. Two surveys of WPAs led to publications describing writing program practice in 1986. Although they were both published by the Modern Language Association, they were prepared independently, using different sources of descriptive data. I discuss them together here because they both assume that descriptions of current practice in themselves provide useful information for those administering writing programs. As Carol Hartzog puts it in her "Conclusion": "I hesitate to make comparisons because comparisons lead toward judgments, and my aim has been not to discover which of these programs is best but to understand how writing programs work and how they suit their universities" (p. 133).

Paul Connolly and Teresa Vilardi have compiled a series of five-page descriptions of twenty-eight writing programs from various kinds of American colleges and universities (the principle of selection is not made clear), with a brief introduction giving no less than fourteen ways in which the teaching of writing is improving. Although the determinedly optimistic tone of the introduction and of the program descriptions becomes a bit hard to take after a while, it is impossible to read the accumulated accounts without a feeling of admiration for the WPAs and their staffs who are responsible for writing instruction in these model institutions. The constantly asserted "success" of the program is supported almost entirely by the opinion of the program director describing his or her achievement; the barely mentioned handicaps of tight budgets, heavy teaching loads, faculty resistance, and the like, pale before the heady statements of theories and influences that have led to a uniquely excellent writing program. Those who have visited numbers of campuses have learned to discount the enthusiasm of WPAs, understandably pleased to have brought about substantial improvements. Nonetheless, even a hardened cynic must see a picture emerge from the collection, one showing the immense difference that a determined WPA can make to both the writing program and the campus climate for writing. A wide variety of writing programs can be implemented to fit the needs of different institutions; and, indeed, each can be seen as successful, according to the situation and criteria of a wide variety of campuses. The most significant strength of a writing program, we hear over and over again, is "its energetic, committed staff members" (p. 28). I have no hesitation in believing it.

The Connolly and Vilardi collection is of limited use, however, since it consists of what I earlier called "show and tell." Presumably, a WPA could find parts of different programs that assertedly work on other campuses and piece together improvements for the home campus, or perhaps simply seek to adopt another campus's program. I find it hard to imagine such borrowings, though, since each of these programs is closely connected to a particular institution. The editors stress the inspirational value of the collection, no mean trait in a field whose vision is often dark: "But a healthy revision of writing instruction within the larger context of general education seems well advanced in many areas of the country. If these models further demonstrate what is possible and spare teachers and students some unnecessary trials and errors, they contribute to that new vision" (p. 5).

Carol Hartzog's survey is based on questionnaires mailed to fifty-two institutions belonging to the Association of American Universities (AAU) and returned by forty-four program directors or department chairs. In addition, she conducted in-person or telephone interviews with thirty-five respondents and visited three campuses. The sample is restricted to major research universities with developed writing programs. (The University of Texas at Austin, we are told, was omitted because of the turmoil its composition program was passing through.) This careful study, focusing on the academic year 1984–85, eschews evaluation and comparison but does aggregate its data in no less than forty-four separate tables. For example, "Table 20: Average Class Size" gives us a range from 14 at Princeton to 25 at Colorado, Boulder; "Table 21: For Whom Are Your Courses, Programs, and Services Designed?" tells us that 42 of the 43 responses list freshmen, 28 list juniors, and 28 list seniors. The first half of the book provides a "composite" of the campus programs surveyed. Seven chapter titles describe what respondents have reported: Profiles of Change; Administrative Structures; Program Directors; The Writing Programs; Faculty and Teaching Assistants; Attitudes, Opinions, and Plans; English and Composition.

The objective descriptiveness of the Hartzog study is moderated by its author's sense of what life is really like on a campus. Thus, instead of giving brief descriptions of her entire sample, she provides in-depth descriptions of just three: the University of North Carolina, Chapel Hill; the University of Pennsylvania; and Harvard University. The clear and wide-ranging portraits of these writing programs show how closely an effective program adapts itself to particular campus needs, even as it profoundly affects the campus climate for writing and learning. The descriptions also show the problems that even these well-funded and highly developed programs must deal with. As the author puts it, she finds it "tempting" to say, "This is what it takes to create a sound writing program and secure its place in the university: a tradition of liberal education; a spirit of educational reform; the support of the administration, the department chair, and faculty members in English, as well as in other departments; grounding in theory and research; association with a successful program; general goodwill; fortunate timing and circumstance; and energetic, creative, solid leadership. Nothing easier. Except in real life." In real life, she points out, "no single model, no single prescription will work in all cases. Most important is the suitability of any single plan, the fit between any program and its university" (p. 12).

The Hartzog book is valuable not only for institutions such as those in its rather elite sample but also for colleges looking for full descriptions of complex writing programs that have helped enrich their campus climates. In its modest way, it offers approaches to writing program organization that can be adopted by any institution. Like the Connolly and Vilardi collection, however, it remains a descriptive resource, to be mined by those seeking applications on their own campuses.

Applying Program Knowledge to the Teaching of Writing

When we look back on a generation of studies about writing programs, we must conclude that the increase of knowledge has been slow and most of the results are repetitive. While Kitzhaber's division of the goals of instruction into "therapy" and "fundamental principles of clear thinking" has been usefully expanded into the patterns of approaches to be examined in the next chapter, we find no clearer consensus now than he did.

The changes anticipated by the accelerated writing research of the last twenty-five years are only slowly working their way into the classroom, where much that is happening (or not happening) would look very familiar to Kitzhaber. However, some changes clearly have taken place in theory, and some of them also have begun to show up in practice.

Perhaps the most obvious development during this time has been in assessment theory and practice. Whereas Kitzhaber assessed the value of composition instruction by means of an elaborate error count, more sophisticated methods of evaluation of actual student writing have now become familiar and almost routine. The satisfactory reliability and the superior validity of direct writing measures have led to much activity in program evaluation, with much useful incidental faculty development. (The California study concludes, after reviewing the frustrated efforts of composition directors to update literature faculty about composition studies, that developing and administering a writing test is the most effective faculty development activity available.) However, as Hillocks (1986) has shown, convincing empirical evidence of student improvement from composition instruction remains exceedingly rare.

We also have signs of the increasing importance, status, professionalism, and effectiveness of the WPA. The widespread commitment to admission of students who in previous generations would not have appeared in college classrooms (most obviously symbolized by the advent of "open enrollment" at the City University of New York in 1970) inevitably increased the size and importance of writing programs and the significance of their administrators. At the same time, a major increase in research on rhetoric and writing led to a new specialization for faculty with substantial practical skills and publication records. Although the scholarship in this field has not attained much status in traditional English departments, the importance of these composition faculty to many departmental writing programs is becoming more and more evident. If recent reports of important shifts in English Ph.D. programs toward writing and rhetoric turn out to be accurate, a professionally active WPA may become an essential part of every up-to-date English department.

It is clearly too early to ask research in composition programs to provide answers to the thorny problems in the field. However, these studies have given us useful ways of thinking about the most significant issues: staffing, curriculum, assessment, pedagogical theories and practices, texts and materials, instructional formats, goals, program structures, and the like. The studies have described in detail a wide variety of model programs, showing the practical range of possible implementation of writing program theory. At the same time, the research has provided a small but useful body of data that can be used to test competing proposals for reform and improvement, and the studies have shown us what seems to be permanent and beyond the reach of changing theory.

Chapter 3

Strengths and Weaknesses
of Approaches
to Teaching Writing

Close observers of American education know that
much is wrong with the teaching of writing in college. Writing
classes are often taught by faculty untrained in the field, using
textbooks bereft of pedagogical concepts, taking class time for
peripheral activities, constructing assignments without clarity of
design or purpose, responding to assignments in unhelpful ways.
The lack of consensus about goals, texts, curriculum, classroom
activities, and standards is apparent even to the most superficial
observer. Furthermore, the measures of success or lack of success are untrustworthy, anecdotal, or impressionistic, and most
teachers and administrators are content to leave them that way,
since they believe that the benefits of the course cannot be
readily defined or measured. Moreover, when statements of goals
are formulated (as they sometimes are for remedial courses), they
usually focus on correctness and mechanics. Emphasis on these
"functional" skills is often naive (at best), ineffective, or more
politically than pedagogically motivated (Ohmann, 1976; Giroux,
1981; Levine, 1982; Rose, 1983; Gould and Heyda, 1986); the
research over the last twenty-five years is almost unanimously
negative about such instruction (Hillocks, 1986, pp. 134–141).

   In spite of these evident weaknesses, there are important
strengths at the center of many writing instruction programs.
Most writing teachers believe in their hearts that their students

improve under their ministrations. Many students also appear to
be convinced of this improvement, since they enroll willingly in
the customary writing courses and even want more of them;
most American universities cannot meet the demand for writing
courses at all levels. This generalized belief that writing courses
are somehow succeeding is widespread enough to represent a
wisdom based on experience. Perhaps the underlying cause of
this continuing felt success is that most institutions place the
teaching of writing in the care of English faculty, a profession
committed to the sensitive use of language, and common sense
suggests that attention to the uses of language is a crucial underlying thread for all successful writing courses. Or perhaps regular writing of any sort, read by an educated reader with some
attention, leads to improvement or, at least, to a feeling that improvement is taking place. Or perhaps, as Thomas Wilcox suggested in 1973, writing classes have the fundamental purpose of
putting a small class of undergraduates in the same room with a
professed intellectual for a few hours a week—a rare and exciting experience for most students, whatever the course design or
result. Recent research has tried to supply some evidence in this
area, but the widespread satisfaction with writing instruction,
despite so much evidence of its insufficiency, presents an interesting puzzle.

I have suggested that one solution to that puzzle is the location of composition within the English department, an arrangement that some composition specialists regard as the main source
of problems with writing programs. These specialists argue that
writing instruction should and will separate, nay divorce, from
its uneasy marriage with literature in the English department.
They also claim that naive teachers of writing may accidentally
stumble into some good pedagogy but that only trained composition faculty can do the job consistently well. I am not persuaded by either claim.

The argument that composition should separate from
English departments has been made with passion by Maxine
Hairston (1985), discussed with scholarly dispassion by Law-
rence Poston (1986), and pursued with ironic logic by Stephen
North (1987), to take only a recent sampling of approaches to

the issue. At such institutions as the University of Southern California, the University of Utah, and Harvard University, the split has taken place to the apparent satisfaction of many (though not all) faculty. Certainly, different kinds of institutions will react in different ways to the possibility of separating composition from English, in accordance with their perceived missions and traditions. But, despite turf and status wars, differing methods of research, new approaches to literacy, and all the other reasons for composition to leave its present home, I think (to use Poston's metaphor) that marriage counseling, not divorce, is the answer.

Perhaps I am extrapolating too much from my own experience with composition faculty outside English, but I think that writing teachers have to be the most sensitive *readers* in the university—that is, those trained to be in the English department. When I watch even well-trained composition faculty from other departments discuss student writing (as I do with some frequency), I keep wanting to call out, "Don't you *see?*" That is, don't you see the thinking not quite completed, the idea asserted but not demonstrated, the insight only half observed, the passive verb destroying the force of the argument, the fine idea buried and half discovered only in the last paragraph, and so on. If college composition is to meet the high calling I set out in the first chapter of this book, it must not become an offshoot of empirical or ethnographic research, a functional set of communicative tools, or any of the several minor disciplines envisioned for it by those frustrated with the failings of present English departments. Without its link to the best writing, composition becomes merely communication; without highly trained readers, the possibility of challenging good writers to become creative thinkers becomes remote; without the present cadre of writing teachers in English departments, doing their work year after year, composition loses its best constituency.

I have considerable faith in the effectiveness of the general run of college English teachers, who seem to be much in need of defense from researchers these days. With the exception of Stephen North, who regards the defeat of "practitioners" by "scholars" and "researchers" as a power shift rather than a clear advance, most composition specialists have little respect for the accumulated "lore" (North's term) that guides teaching practice. While I have no respect for ignorance or for the foolish repetition of workbook formulas that some teachers mistake for instruction in writing, I have a great deal of respect for much of the teaching of writing that my English colleagues do. A pedagogy based on a human concern for students and a serious respect for the possibilities of the written word, enriched by literary sensitivity and advanced education, is not likely to go far wrong. Indeed, the most elaborate and successful of all in-service teacher training programs, the National Writing Project (based on the Bay Area Writing Project), takes as its fundamental assumption the high value of the earned knowledge of classroom teachers: teachers sharing with other teachers their best practice. Perhaps today's wisdom and tomorrow's research findings still have something to learn from the accumulated (if unstructured) practice of many yesterdays.

Patterns of Composition Instruction:
The California Construct

The following description of patterns of composition instruction is derived from the analysis of replies to the questionnaire collected by the California project (White and Polin, 1986). Since this project claims to provide an accurate picture of the way that writing is now being taught at the college level, we need to say a few words about how the data were collected, who supplied the information, and how the information was analyzed. After reviewing those procedures, we will examine each of the patterns, with an eye to the strengths and weaknesses of each.

As mentioned in Chapter Two, the questionnaire was devised by the project's research team to elicit as much information as possible from those teaching remedial and regular composition courses on the nineteen campuses of the California State University (CSU) during the calendar year 1982. Despite the elaborateness of the twelve-page questionnaire, the project achieved a 56 percent rate of return, allowing the researchers to claim that the 418 completed documents constituted a representative sample of the CSU and of composition teachers at the college level in general. The CSU, with its wide diversity of campus types, environments, populations, and programs, is roughly representative of most public and private institutions of higher education in the United States. The principal difference between the CSU sample and the composition faculty at many other institutions is the general integration of composition instruction into the teaching responsibilities of the regular English department: only 5.4 percent of the sample were graduate teaching assistants, and about 60 percent of the respondents reported completion of the Ph.D.

The researchers did not begin with presumed groupings or categories; instead, they proceeded inductively, allowing the statistical operation of factor analysis to provide patterns of responses on questionnaire items. After the data analysis produced the six groupings of responses, the research team attempted to understand, name, and explain the meaning of the patterns so generated. This procedure gave the researchers not only a description but also a measure for assessing who holds which instructional beliefs in each of three instructional contexts: remedial, freshman composition, and other lower-division writing courses. Of the 418 respondents, 233 chose to report on their freshman composition course instruction, 74 referenced their remedial coursework, and 64 described instruction in other lower-division writing courses they teach; 47 neglected to mark their course referent and were excluded from the analyses. Of the 74 who referenced their remedial coursework, the majority (43) were not tenure-track instructors. Of the 233 describing their freshman composition course, more than half (132) were tenured/tenure-track. Of the 64 teaching "other lower-division writing courses," the majority (44) were tenured/tenure track.

A Multifaceted View of Writing Instruction

Most of the items on the questionnaire asked respondents to reflect on their instructional practices in teaching remedial writing, first-term freshman composition, or some other lower-division writing course. After indicating course referent, all respondents answered the same set of items on their classroom instructional practices and goals.

In constructing the questionnaire items on instruction, the researchers wanted to avoid relying on one or two answers to a multiple-choice item to describe what was going on in composition classrooms. They decided on a multifaceted approach, partitioning instruction into six categories: (1) themes underlying the organization and sequence of writing class instruction, (2) materials used in writing class instruction, (3) classroom teaching arrangements in writing classes, (4) kind and number of writing assignments required of writing class students, (5) frequency of various kinds of responses to student writing, and (6) proportion of in-class time spent in each of a variety of activities.

Themes. The questionnaire provided eleven theme statements for respondents to rate in terms of importance to course instruction ("very important" to "not important at all"). These theme statements represented a variety of perspectives, such as "Expose students to good literature," "Allow for practice in writing activities necessary for success in other college courses," "Teach invention skills, such as planning, prewriting, clustering, heuristics," and "Allow for in-class writing in a workshop setting." Many respondents rated more than one theme "very important."

Materials. The questionnaire offered faculty a list of eleven kinds of materials that can be used in support of writing instruction. These varied from grammar handbooks to students' own writings. As with instructional themes, respondents rated the importance of each item.

Classroom Arrangements. The questionnaire offered four items describing instructor-student interaction and asked respondents to rate the frequency with which they engaged in each. Types of interaction included small-group and individualized work, formal lectures, and guided discussions (for example, "Simultaneous small-group activities, during which I circulate among the working groups"). Choices of frequency ranged along a four-point scale from "almost always" to "rarely or never." Faculty also were asked to indicate the underlying reason for these choices.

In-Class Activities. The questionnaire provided a list of fourteen in-class activities that might reasonably occur in support of writing instruction: writing "on a given topic" or "topics of their own choosing" or "free writing or journal writing"; discussing "upcoming assignments" or "mechanics and standard usage" or "linguistics"; and others. This section required a combined measure of emphasis and frequency. The researchers recognized that particular class activities might be concentrated at the beginning of a term or dispersed across the term, recurring on and off as part of a class session. The questionnaire contained a rating system that took these differences into account and yet provided some sense of range from "not done in class" or "not done at all" to "a major activity in every class."

Assignments and Responses. The questionnaire presented four kinds of writing assignments (paragraph, multiparagraph essay, report, and research paper) and asked how many of each were required. Additionally, seven types of responses (from letter grade to request for major revision) were listed. Oddly enough, there was very little variation among faculty in their reports of their writing assignments and of their responses to student writing. This lack of variation in answers made it impossible to find distinguishing "patterns" of responses, and, thus, impossible for these items to be strongly linked with one or another of the patterns of instructional themes, materials, arrangements, or activities. Virtually all respondents reported that they assigned substantial quantities of writing to their students and spent substantial amounts of time responding to that writing, both on the papers and in person. If this report is to be believed (although it is a self-report, it does correspond with common anecdotal knowledge), it may provide an answer to the underlying student belief in the effectiveness of writing instruction courses in general: as long as faculty are requiring and responding to regular student writing, the underlying goals of writing instruction are being met.

Six Patterns of Instruction

Responses to themes, materials, teaching arrangements, and in-class activities combined to form six instructional factors. The researchers called each factor an instructional "approach" to teaching writing and selected specific factor names to represent the broad instructional theme characterized by the items the factor encompasses. The six patterns of instruction represented by these factors are listed in Table 1.

The numbers in the "Item Weight" columns represent the relative strength of each questionnaire item as a member of that factor group. The higher the weight, the more confidence one can have in it as a characteristic of that trait. Items with lower weights are relatively less reliable indicators of the trait. The report included in the factors all items whose weights indicate at least a moderate influence (weights at and above .35). For example, of the six questionnaire items comprising the literature approach, "Analyzing literature" has the highest item weight (.82), which indicates that it is the most stable and, therefore, the most characteristic element of the trait.

Table 1. Six Approaches to Writing Instruction.

1. Literature Approach

Questionnaire Item	Item Weight
Instructional Theme:	
To expose students to good literature	.70
Instructional Materials:	
Poetry and fiction anthologies	.68
Poetry, fiction, and nonfiction anthologies	.64
Individual works of literature	.71
Class Activities:	
Analyzing literature	.82
Analyzing prose models of composition	.35

2. Peer Workshop Approach

Questionnaire Item	Item Weight
Instructional Theme:	
To teach invention skills, such as planning, prewriting, clustering, heuristics	.42
To provide regular in-class writing in a workshop setting	.37
Instructional Materials:	
Students' own writing	.42

Table 1. Six Approaches to Writing Instruction, Cont'd.

Classroom Arrangements:	
Simultaneous small-group activities, during which I circulate among the working groups	.66
Class Activities:	
Free writing or journal writing	.52
Students discussing or scoring their own writing	.72
Students working with other students	.82

3. Individualized Writing Lab Approach

Questionnaire Item	Item Weight
Instructional Theme:	
To allow for frequent in-class writing	.79
To provide regular in-class writing in a workshop setting	.59
Classroom Arrangements:	
Individual work, permitting me to circulate among working students	.47
Class Activities:	
Writing essays on a given topic	.50
Working with tutors during class	.41

4. Text-Based Rhetoric Approach

Questionnaire Item	Item Weight
Instructional Theme:	
To proceed developmentally through discourse modes (for example, from description to persuasion)	.51
Instructional Materials:	
Nonfiction anthology	.63
Rhetoric text or style book, without handbook	.49
Rhetoric text or style book, handbook included	.56
Class Activities:	
Working on or discussing material in texts on composition	.61
Analyzing prose models of composition	.56

5. Basic Skills Approach

Questionnaire Item	Item Weight
Instructional Theme:	
To teach for competence with basic units of prose (for example, phrase, sentence, paragraph)	.51
To teach correct grammar and usage	.69

(continued on next page)

Table 1. Six Approaches to Writing Instruction, Cont'd.

Instructional Materials:	
Grammar and usage handbook	.46
Class Activities:	
Discussing mechanics and standard usage	.65

6. Service Course Approach

Questionnaire Item	Item Weight
Instructional Theme:	
To practice writing activities necessary for success in other college courses (for example, term papers)	.65
Kinds of Writing Assignments:	
Writing a term paper or research paper	.74
Class Activities:	
Discussing techniques for writing research papers	.76

Strengths and Weaknesses of the Approaches

Literature Approach. The main thrust of the literature approach is classroom analysis of literature. The reading assignments are works of literature, class time is spent discussing the literature, and the instructional theme is "to expose students to good literature." This approach has been under attack since the early years of this century but nonetheless continues to thrive—primarily because most faculty who teach writing have passed through graduate programs in literature, and that is what these teachers know best. Some of them may have received informal or even formal instruction in composition, but many who use this approach remain unaware or unconvinced that there is anything else appropriate to do in a college-level English class. There are also some faculty who have strong theoretical and historical reasons for selecting this approach to the teaching of writing.

The literature approach is deeply embedded in the more selective universities, where its most eloquent defenders reside. On such campuses, the approach is so identified with academic virtue that changes are exceedingly unlikely. One Ivy League college, for example, found that its usual freshman composition course, based on Milton's *Paradise Lost*, seemed inappropriate for the nontraditional students it had lately begun to admit as part of its student affirmative action program. Despite some misgivings about letting down standards, the college established a remedial writing course, using basic reading matter more attuned, so the faculty felt, to the needs of ill-prepared unconventional students: Milton's shorter poem "Samson Agonistes."

Most institutions have a wider range of possibilities for their writing curriculum, and on some of these campuses debate about the literature approach tends to be tense, even vitriolic, since the issue reflects a deep division within the field of English. Most English departments are dominated by literary scholars, who often have little respect for or interest in the teaching of writing, while those most involved with the teaching of writing tend to be relatively powerless and less secure. Thus, the debate often involves such problems as faculty status (many tenure committees do not count teaching or even scholarship in composition as sufficiently professional work), academic standards (can reading and writing about nonliterary topics be sufficiently demanding?), and social class (is the traditional literary canon appropriate for nontraditional students?). And since the lower-status composition teaching is more time consuming and emotionally demanding than the teaching of literature and often supports financially the advanced work in literature, the resentments and defensiveness that surround the entire subject overshadow pedagogical debate. Those who oppose the literature approach argue that it represents an avoidance of the faculty's responsibility to teach the material and students of today's world. Those who espouse the approach insist that it transmits a culture to a student body increasingly in need of it and decreasingly aware of it.

We need to detach this approach from these other arguments if we are to assess its strengths and weaknesses. The question is not all that complicated: To what degree should a writing course attend to the study of literature?

One strength that is beyond dispute is the force of tradition. Literature entered the curriculum as a way to teach grammar; it provided late medieval and Renaissance education with pleasing and instructive examples of good writing to be copied and imitated. For five centuries, the literature approach held sway, and beside it other approaches are new and untested. Testimonials to its power are everywhere. Closely allied to the force of tradition is the strength of prose models. Since literature is language used at its most sophisticated (the argument goes), writing students will profit from close and regular attention to the language of literature as a model to strive toward. And since the study of literature is valuable in its own right, a writing curriculum based on literature is doubly valuable—both for what it is and for the model it presents. Furthermore, the literature is eminently worth writing about and thus provides writing topics and material for student thought, discussion, and composition. Since composition classes at the college level require content and intellectual challenge as well as practice in skills, the study of literature is appropriate, natural, and beneficial to students as well as faculty.

The weaknesses of the approach have to do with both its assumptions and its applications. It is by no means clear that the study of prose models from literature teaches students much or anything about writing. The prose models intended as examples are likely to seem irrelevant and unreachable to the students, many of whom are still struggling for elementary clarity and coherence; the sophistication of the literature is so far beyond the abilities of most students that it can only serve to confirm a sense of inadequacy. Indeed, the very attractiveness of the literature as a study in its own right is usually taken to be the principal weakness of this approach, since it not only allows but actually urges everyone involved to put aside attention to student writing in favor of the more delightful literature. Those most opposed to this approach do not see it as an approach to teaching writing at all; they see it as a seductive way to avoid such teaching by substituting a wholly different activity. Students in these classes may wind up knowing more about poetry or fiction or Shakespeare, but there is no evidence that such knowledge will improve student writing.

The literature approach fell into disrepute under these attacks and in response to student cries for truth in advertising during the 1960s. But it never wholly died, since traditional faculty were often dismayed at the approaches that replaced it. Their claims about the connection between reading and writing ability have not been disproved, and their call for academic content in the freshman course has been renewed. Writing classes without reading material beyond duplicated student essays or such popular sources as newspapers or magazines may force attention to the student writing, but both the challenge and the quality of such courses seem sharply diminished. Those favoring this approach admit that it can be abused; but they argue that it requires as much student writing, and focuses as much attention on that writing, as other approaches do.

Peer Workshop Approach. Small-group activities and arrangements are the critical elements of the peer workshop approach: students working with other students, in small groups, discussing or scoring their own writing. Instructors committed to this approach provide prewriting activities, allow for writing on a topic of one's own choosing, and use student writing as instructional material in such activities as peer criticism and scoring.

The particular advantage of this approach is that it expands the audience for student writing beyond the teacher. Many students will in fact produce more careful work if it is to be read by their peers, particularly in a class setting where these peers have received training in responding constructively to writing. Students who become accustomed to helping their peers with their writing will, the argument goes, internalize these methods for themselves as well. The workshop setting also provides a congenial environment for writing, particularly for students who may not be accustomed to the concentration and steady revision required for good work. Since constructive support (rather than more or less distant criticism) and suggestions for revision (rather than simple judgment of the product) are usual in these workshops, students learn about the writing process, and the teacher is at hand to help them apply what they learn. Attention is wholly focused on the students' writing, without distractions from outside reading; and the students will be interested in and concerned about their work, since they have selected the subjects that they write about. Furthermore, the training in group work is excellent preparation for the collaborative writing that is the norm in much writing outside the university setting.

This approach to writing instruction is much in fashion these days, not only because of these strengths but because of the generally pleasant tone of such classes. The teacher becomes a coach and a guide, rather than an adversary or a judge, and the students are required to become active participants in their own and others' learning. An added benefit to the students is the immediate response they receive to their work; an added benefit to the faculty is relief from the extra hours of paper grading that traditionally burden the writing teacher's evenings and weekends. Not surprisingly, many teachers are so committed to this method that they regard it as the only right and proper way to teach writing.

Nonetheless, this approach has some clear weaknesses. The most obvious is the relative lack of content for the course. Those who raise this objection insist that writing is more than a mere skill; it involves the consideration of new concepts and great books. Writers need to consider their ideas in the context of other writers and thinkers. If writers are restricted only to what they think they know, they will be constricted rather than liberated by their writing courses. This approach does not expose students to the range of thinking and writing that is traditional for the freshman English course and therefore is more appropriate for a trade school than for a university. The apparent good feeling in peer workshop courses, opponents will argue, is a sign that the instructor has abandoned an important part of a writing teacher's responsibilities: to challenge students to learn more than they think they want, to insist that they can do better than they think they can.

Individualized Writing Lab Approach. At first glance, the individualized writing lab approach seems to describe the same instructional environment as the peer workshop approach, though only one questionnaire item is shared between them: "To provide regular in-class writing in a workshop setting." In the context of items comprising the peer workshop factor, the notion of "workshop" describes a variety of small-group activities. On the other hand, the items comprising the individualized writing lab approach reflect an emphasis on the individual, providing a setting in which the course instructor or a tutor works with student writers by themselves. This factor does not include questionnaire items describing in-class discussion or instructional materials. Instead, most items emphasize "doing" writing in class.

This approach has been widely used in community colleges, following its popularization by the late Roger Garrison, who gave many seminars teaching its applications (1981). But many teachers at all levels have been attracted by its ease of use and its immediate effectiveness in getting reluctant students to write. The essential strength of this approach depends on steady in-class writing on an appropriate assigned topic, with the teacher circulating as an editorial coach, giving two or three minutes of commentary to each student each class. If it is argued that writing requires more time than is available in class, proponents will point to evidence that the average college freshman spends only eight to ten hours each week preparing for *all* classes (see the depressing national student surveys put together by Alexander Astin, published in the *Chronicle of Higher Education* in January of each year); students writing two to three hours a week in class are at least doing that much work and, in addition, are receiving an immediate response that often leads to some revision.

This approach also has the benefit of reducing the writing teacher's work load to that of instructors in other fields, since no papers need be taken home for reading. But the teacher must work very hard during the class hour to be certain of giving a useful response to each student's writing. Assignments must be carefully structured so that they can be managed in the restricted time allowed. The essential fact of writing must be reduced, according to this approach, to the individual writer wrestling with the blank sheet of paper. Everything else is a distraction.

The weaknesses of this approach are similar to those of the previous approach. It has no place for reading or even much reflection and cannot accommodate such longer tasks as a research paper. If it teaches writing skill, as its proponents claim, the skill it teaches is a restricted and functional one, without much concern for writing as discovery or development of ideas. To teach writing without a context of reading and challenging ideas, opponents insist, is to delude students into thinking that they know all they need to know already; writing then becomes a mechanical skill, not an intellectual discipline.

Text-Based Rhetoric Approach. The text-based rhetoric approach to instruction relies heavily on rhetoric textbooks and what publishers call "rhetoric readers"—that is, anthologies arranged according to rhetorical categories. These books provide models of writing and style guidelines, and they are used to generate class discussion, generally in the form of analysis of prose models exemplifying the several kinds of writing that are to be taught. This factor does not include student writing in class. Instead, students spend a good deal of class time reading and analyzing other people's writing, learning from increasingly sophisticated examples.

The great popularity of this approach is attested to by the constant flow of textbooks designed for it. These books generally include a wide variety of essays and other nonfiction prose, often arranged according to one rhetorical theory or another, with alternate tables of contents rearranging the selections according to one or more competing theories. The analysis of professional writing that takes up much of the class time attempts to connect the student writing assignments with the reading assignments, as well as to raise ideas and problems for discussion. Furthermore, there is often a developmental pattern involved in this approach, embodied in writing and reading assignments that proceed from the relatively easy to the more difficult.

The strengths of this approach lie chiefly in the close relationship between the reading and the writing required. In general, the essays are eminently worth reading and discussing, introducing students (and often their graduate student teachers) to interesting ideas from a variety of fields. The textbooks normally offer such a wide selection of readings that almost any teacher, whatever his or her particular interests, can design an interesting sequence with interesting writing assignments from them. Courses using this approach are not bound to the rhetorical theory half-heartedly espoused by the text but generally allow instructors to choose or create some theory of their own to structure the course. The writing is done out of class, as is the grading of papers by the instructor.

The weaknesses of the approach stem from failures to connect the reading with the writing (a link much more readily seen by instructors than by their students) and from the theoretical uncertainty of the rhetorical structures. The most popular of such structures remains the four-part division generally attributed to the nineteenth-century American rhetorician Alexander Bain (1866; see also Harned, 1985, and, particularly, the bibliographical discussion by D'Angelo, 1987). Bain described four rhetorical "modes" as Descriptive, Narrative, Expository, and Persuasive; despite a century of reevaluation and refinement by modern rhetoricians, these outmoded and inconsistent categories have achieved a kind of permanency among textbooks and for some teachers through repeated use. Other modal structures have been put forward with considerable frequency and passion: the heuristic (that is, problem-solving) patterns of Young, Becker, and Pike (1970); the interdisciplinary modes of writing-across-the-curriculum advocates; the process-oriented structures of those concerned with the way writers turn out texts; and so on. The variety of rhetorical theories and the complexity of some of them (see, for instance, Kinneavy, 1971) have allowed for distinctions among the textbooks, which tend to have many readings in common; one can find readers in which Bain's four modes are divided and subdivided into so many supposed "modes" of writing that each week of the term can deal with a separate one.

As with the literature approach, this method of teaching is subject to abuse by teachers who would rather teach the content of the reading than deal with student writing. Class time may focus on the ideas or style of the reading rather than the problems of the student writers. And weaker students are likely to have enough trouble handling the reading to keep them from getting under way as writers.

Basic Skills Approach. The basic skills approach emphasizes writing as "correct" expression and seeks to establish in students the fundamentals of sentence and paragraph construction. The reading material tends to be restricted to a grammar and usage handbook, and class time is spent on discussions of writing mechanics and problems of usage.

Despite twenty-five years of research demonstrating the futility of this approach to the teaching of writing at any level (Hillocks, 1986, pp. 133–151), it lingers on at the college level (as it does in the schools much more prominently), mainly in courses designated as remedial. Teachers or program directors unaware of the research and of more effective methods of teaching resort to the workbooks, usage handbooks, and the like, in the belief that these "basics" will be learned if they are taught once again, and will somehow be applied if they are learned. This approach persists among teachers who do not know what else to do and among those who associate it with such intellectual disciplines as learning irregular Latin verbs. Its pedagogical virtue, if it can be called a virtue, is that it fills up class time and provides student assignments; it gives both teacher and student the illusion that something useful is going on. The weakness is not only that the method does not work but that (by using time that could be spent in writing and reading) it actually interferes with student learning.

Service Course Approach. The service course approach regards college composition as a general education requirement whose principal purpose is to prepare students for writing in their other college courses. Writing assignments and in-class activities revolve around the term or research paper.

This approach has strong defenders among faculty who see writing as a tool for learning in all disciplines. In their view, the writing course should give students control over this tool and not waste time by attending to writing for its own sake or to generalized good reading. Proponents of this approach are often impatient with what they take to be the usual approach by English teachers, with their supposed emphasis on belles lettres and "flowery writing" and their insufficient attention to the practical needs of student writing. Those who espouse this strong pragmatic approach are not opposed to reading or to the use of writing as a means of learning, but they define writing as research, a device for discovering and conveying information.

The strengths of this approach derive from its focus and its practical orientation. Since students know that other courses are likely to demand similar work, they are strongly motivated to learn how to do it well. The focus on conducting research, taking and organizing notes, constructing footnotes and bibliographies, and so on, is purposeful and useful. Most students have considerable difficulty in learning how to make clear summaries of others' ideas; the problem of using quotations honestly—to support one's own ideas rather than to substitute for such ideas—is probably the most difficult of writing problems for college students. Furthermore, since students normally select the topic for research from areas of their special interest, and have a genuine need to know more about their subject, they are well motivated to pursue this difficult task. Thus, this approach takes for its central concern the most practical kind of writing for college students, provides a clear motivation for learning, and seeks to address the complex and difficult problems of such writing.

Despite these strengths, the service course approach is not much used and has never been much in fashion. In the first place, many writing teachers believe that writing should not be regarded as merely a tool for other purposes; writing, they insist, is important in its own right and has many functions beyond merely summarizing information. Writing should help students discover who they are and what they think, as well as what is lying in the library. Particularly at the freshman level, the research paper is often an empty exercise, with students going through the motions of an activity without context, background, or meaning. Real research requires substantial background knowledge before a student can identify serious issues in a field and can distinguish the significant from the trivial or the merely popular. College freshmen cannot be expected to have this kind of background. Thus, the problems that are the subjects of research tend toward the superficial (the history and importance of some rock musician is a common topic), the papers tend to be long strings of quotations not always acknowledged as such, and there is a thriving market in the sale of used research papers for those unwilling to go through all the necessary motions just to get a grade. Furthermore, real research varies considerably from field to field, and not merely in format or citation style; therefore, the argument goes, it is the proper business of the academic major to teach research in its field.

Many writing courses do pay some attention to research, and a small research paper is a frequent assignment whatever the approach. But courses devoted wholly to the service approach seem generally unattractive to most writing teachers, who believe that its weaknesses outweigh its strengths.

Conclusions from the California Study

After this brief survey of approaches to the teaching of writing, it is natural to ask which is best. The California team set out to find answers to that question but felt that they had insufficient evidence to draw such conclusions. Since each approach has advocates and practitioners (as well as opponents), and since each institution has its own mix of program, students, faculty, and tradition, it is risky or worse to attempt a simple answer to such a question. There is no single best approach to the teaching of writing under all circumstances and with all students.

The California research shows that individual faculty members favor one or another of these approaches and then use that approach to teach writing at whatever level. We could then say that the best approach to the teaching of writing is whatever approach works best for an individual teacher, but such a statement would be too superficial. Faculty members select an approach out of a set of trained beliefs about the nature of writing, the capacities and interests of their students, the purposes of the general education program on their campus, their own strengths and weaknesses as people and teachers, and many other components. Some unconsciously adopt approaches chosen by others (perhaps even those who taught them writing in high school) and are not aware that other possibilities exist; they may defend an approach simply because they are used to it and believe in it. People are generally reluctant to abandon a familiar methodology if they perceive it to work. Since each approach has both strong and weak points, we cannot construct a compelling argument for one of them.

Nonetheless, we need not remain in a state of pure anarchy. I, for example, am firmly committed to the text-based rhetoric approach, because that approach works best for me and my students at my institution. In *Teaching and Assessing Writing* (White, 1985, pp. 251-289), I set out a curriculum that embodies a coherent plan for teaching certain kinds of writing, even while claiming (properly) that my plan might not be right for many others. Although we cannot reasonably expect to conclude what is best for everyone, we can expect writing teachers to know what they are doing in the writing class, and why. Not every writing teacher will write a book explaining his or her procedures, though sometimes it seems as if every other one has, but every teacher should be able to explain to colleagues and students the theory and rationale behind the classroom practice.

Patterns of Composition Instruction:
The Hillocks Construct

The same year that the California research was published, a long-awaited and eagerly expected book appeared as a joint venture of the National Conference on Research in English and the ERIC Clearinghouse on Reading and Communication Skills: *Research on Written Composition: New Directions for Teaching,* by George Hillocks, Jr. (1986). This study (which updates an earlier study by Braddock, Lloyd-Jones, and Schoer, 1963) reviews and evaluates empirical research over the preceding twenty-five years, establishes an extensive bibliography of such work (pp. 253-355), and makes strong recommendations about preferred methods of composition instruction. It employs the new statistical device of meta-analysis in order to group studies for greater generalizability and employs a forbidding technical language to amass statistical evidence for its positions. Since the study makes recommendations in the same areas as the California study, in what Hillocks calls "modes of instruction" and "foci of instruction," the two projects complement each other in interesting ways.

Despite its impressive parentage and quantity of data, the

section of the Hillocks study that looks at approaches to teaching writing has been under attack on several grounds: sampling, terminology, and recommendations. (The California study has not received such attack, probably because it is not well known and makes much more modest claims.) The sampling problem comes from the method of meta-analysis, which makes particularly severe demands on its data. Since studies must be parallel to be grouped, and since they must share certain similar characteristics (such as control groups and reliable measures of writing quality), most of the over five hundred studies in the Hillocks sample had to be excluded from meta-analysis. Only sixty could be used, and of these only twenty-three were used for the meta-analysis of modes—and twelve of the twenty-three were unpublished dissertations. In addition, most of the studies were based on younger children rather than college students. To be sure, the sixty surviving studies included 6,313 students in experimental groups and 5,392 in control groups (p. 187), a respectable sample size for most generalizations. Nonetheless, Hillocks is careful to state the limitations of the data and, indeed, argues throughout that the next generation of researchers must be more systematic and clear.

In explaining the terminology for his modes of instruction, Hillocks cites one of his earlier studies "of three modes of instruction in freshman English classes at a large midwestern university. On the basis of classroom observations and interviews, researchers classified instructors as presentational, nondirectional, or environmental" (p. 116). An attitude survey, he continues, showed "highly significant differences ($p < .0001$) among students taught in the three modes on eleven factors examined." Since the categories seemed clear, he retained the terms *presentational* and *environmental*, renamed the nondirectional mode the *natural process* mode, and added an *individualized* mode. This odd and confusing terminology has troubled even sympathetic readers (for example, Larson, 1987), but the presentation of these "modes" along with the less problematic "foci of instruction" does give us one of the few windows into the writing classroom, asking us to look closely at approaches to the teaching of writing, to examine the assumptions behind them, and to compare their results. Hillocks also uses data to support his discussion, evaluation, and (for once) recommendations about approaches to composition instruction.

Four Modes of Instruction

Presentational. The presentational mode "is characterized by (1) relatively clear and specific objectives, e.g., to use particular rhetorical techniques; (2) lecture and teacher-led discussion dealing with concepts to be learned and applied; (3) the study of models and other materials which explain and illustrate the concept; (4) specific assignments or exercises which generally involve imitating a pattern or following rules that have been previously discussed; and (5) feedback following the writing, coming primarily from teachers" (pp. 116–117). In his later analysis of this mode, which he calls "the most common and widespread," Hillocks notes that "the instructor dominates all activity, with students acting as the passive recipients of rules, advice, and examples of good writing." Not surprisingly, he finds this mode "the least effective mode examined" (p. 247).

Natural Process. Hillocks defines "natural process" (an idiosyncratic term, not to be confused with "the writing process") as "characterized by (1) generalized objectives, e.g., to increase fluency and skill in writing; (2) free writing about whatever interests the students, either in a journal or as a way of 'exploring a subject'; (3) writing for audiences of peers; (4) generally positive feedback from peers; (5) opportunities to revise and rework writing; and (6) high levels of interaction among students" (p. 119). "The instructor encourages students to write for other students, to receive comments from them, and to revise their drafts in light of comments from both students and the instructor. But the instructor does not plan activities to help develop specific strategies of composing." Hillocks presents data to show that this mode is "about 50 percent more effective than the presentational mode" but still "about 25 percent less effective than the average experimental treatment [that is, the average gain made by all students in all experiments that Hillocks included]" (p. 247).

Individualized. Hillocks has relatively little to say about the individualized mode, in which "students receive instruction through tutorials, programmed materials of some kind, or a combination of the two" (p. 126). The data are slim and unclear (pp. 126–128), but the mode appears to be about as effective as the natural process mode (p. 247).

Environmental. The environmental mode, the mode that Hillocks prefers, appears to share the advantages of both the natural process and the presentational modes without their disadvantages. It is "characterized by (1) clear and specific objectives, e.g., to increase the use of specific detail and figurative language; (2) materials and problems selected to engage students with each other in specifiable processes important to some particular aspect of writing; and (3) activities, such as small-group problem-centered discussions, conducive to high levels of peer interaction concerning specific tasks. Teachers in this mode, in contrast to the presentational mode, are likely to minimize lecture and teacher-led discussion. Rather, they structure activities so that, while teachers may provide brief introductory lectures, students work on particular tasks in small groups before proceeding to similar tasks independently" (p. 122).

Hillocks calls this mode *environmental* "because it brings teacher, student, and materials more nearly into balance and, in effect, takes advantage of all resources of the classroom." This mode is effective because it places "priority on high levels of student involvement" and "on structured problem-solving activities, with clear objectives." The data are compelling: "On pre-to-post measures, the environmental mode is over four times more effective than the traditional presentational mode and three times more effective than the natural process mode" (p. 247).

Foci of Instruction

There is less difficulty with the "foci of instruction," which Hillocks defines with great precision: "Foci of instruction include types of content or activities which teachers of composition expect to have a salutary effect on writing. These include the study of traditional grammar, work with mechanics, the study of model compositions to identify features of good writing, sentence combining, inquiry, and free writing" (p. 204). While the California factor analysis combined what it called "instructional themes" into the multifaceted view of writing instruction that yielded its six approaches, Hillocks considers each "focus" separately and makes recommendations on each.

When he evaluates the different foci of instruction, Hillocks has no surprises. Traditional school grammar "has no effect on raising the quality of student writing" (p. 248). The only measurable effects were, in fact, negative ones. The conclusion is clear: "School boards, administrators, and teachers who impose the systematic study of traditional school grammar on their students over lengthy periods of time in the name of teaching writing do them a gross disservice which should not be tolerated by anyone concerned with the effective teaching of good writing. We need to learn how to teach standard usage and mechanics after careful task analysis and with minimal grammar" (pp. 248–249).

Teaching from models is significantly more useful than the study of grammar but less effective than the other techniques looked at. So is free writing, "only about two-thirds as effective as the average experimental treatment" (p. 249). Sentence combining turns out to be twice as effective as free writing in enhancing the quality of student writing, as is the use of scales and criteria in class, if students internalize them. However, we should note, as Hillocks does not, Joseph Comprone's (1987, p. 306) warning about sentence-combining data: "Sentence-combining research, focused as it has been on syntactical units at the expense of whole discourse, has suffered from the problems that occur when language is studied and used in decontextualized forms. Students learn to do linguistic tricks, to make longer and more embedded but not necessarily better sentences." In any event, the winner on all counts is what Hillocks calls "inquiry," which has to do with the use of details to convey personal experience and to develop and support generalizations; "inquiry" also has to do with critical thinking, problem solving, and development of argument. Not surprisingly, this attention to writing as discovery and thinking turns out to be "nearly four times more effective than free writing and over two-and-a-half times more powerful than the traditional study of model pieces of writing" (p. 249).

Conclusions from the Hillocks Study

Despite the weight and prominence of the Hillocks study, I find the California research more reflective of reality and more useful. (But then I was principal investigator for the California project, so my view is bound to be somewhat partial.) Two of Hillocks's "modes" seem to correspond to the California "approaches": the individual mode is similar to the individualized writing lab approach, and the natural process mode is rather like the peer workshop approach. But these similarities begin to fade when we look at the way the instructors describe what they do in the California model. The presentational mode, which is (according to Hillocks) very bad, and the environmental mode, which is very good, have only a tenuous similarity to the other four approaches that CSU faculty use. Perhaps the literature approach tends toward the presentational, though there is nothing essentially "presentational" (in the negative Hillocks sense) in analyzing literature, and perhaps the text-based rhetoric approach and the service course approach are environmental, since they both explicitly include classroom discussion. But the fit is uncomfortable because Hillocks's modes do not seem based on what college English teachers actually do. All teachers will regard themselves as "environmental," since that category encompasses the best teaching techniques. The other modes seem to be arbitrarily constructed and limited straw men (or straw modes), neglecting the different virtues of different teaching and learning styles. Part of the problem with meta-analysis, as Stephen Witte (1987a, p. 206) acutely observes in his review of Hillocks's book, is that it "minimizes what are often important differences across studies and accentuates only their similarities."

Nonetheless, the Hillocks book is bound to have a great deal of influence, though I think it has more to say to researchers in the field than it does to teachers. It tells writing teachers to avoid lectures, school grammar, and undirected or pointless assignments—which will not be news to the teachers likely to read it. But it has important and new ideas for those involved in writing research. The research community needs to have much more rigorous standards for its own work and much more careful generalizations when it uses that work to form recommendations to teachers.

Knowledge, Choices, and Power

When we step back to consider what all this research has to tell us about the teaching of writing in college, some general and helpful outlines become clear. In the first place, it is obvious that every teacher is working within the constraints of a writing program; many choices in relation to writing instruction are in fact determined by the program. Nonetheless, within those constraints, every teacher must make choices about the instructional approach to take, the particular assignments to give, the degree of authority to keep or distribute to peer groups, the kinds of responses to make to student writing, the underlying themes of the writing class—in short, the constant, continuing series of professional decisions that form a teacher's working life. Those who are not aware of the range of choices available, and what research has to say about the strengths and weaknesses of those choices, are not in control of their professional lives. The decisions they should be making are being made by others, sometimes by such shadowy figures as long-dead grade school teachers whose imprint is almost indelible. Many school teachers (who rarely encounter writing research), for example, find themselves liberated when they hear that research findings have invalidated school grammar as an effective teaching device (though these findings were old news twenty-five years ago); these teachers were not, I hear after every workshop, aware that they could do what they really thought was best in a writing class.

Knowledge thus is in fact power. We do not by any means know all we should about the teaching of writing. But we know a great deal more than most teachers dream of applying to their own teaching. We also know enough about how the most effective teachers work to make a few useful generalizations. We are not entirely free, of course, constrained as we are by our campus programs; but most teachers can use what we know to change their teaching for the better.

Chapter 4

Teaching Writing Within the Undergraduate Curriculum

The place of writing at the center of the liberal arts undergraduate curriculum derives from its double role as a socializing discipline (enforcing and confirming student membership in an educated community) and as an individualizing discipline (demanding critical thinking and an active relation of the self to material under study). While both of these functions are important, the second one is more significant for the undergraduate curriculum. That is, writing instruction becomes a *liberating* activity—and hence properly an essential part of the liberal arts—when it demands and rewards thinking for oneself. When we look closely at the undergraduate program most American students pursue, with its fragmented view of knowledge and its emphasis on the accumulation of information, writing emerges as a unifying and integrating force. Writing, as an active form of critical thinking, demands that students make sense of what they think they know. But such writing never comes easily to students and is much harder to teach than the conventions of discourse.

The teaching of creativity and independent thinking has never been easy or comfortable, and in contemporary America it has become particularly controversial and risky. Social critics point to the refined management and manipulation of popular opinion in our time, government secrecy, and incredible armaments as signs that a truly informed and independent populace is the last thing our society now demands, though the first thing it really needs. Sometimes the version of "literacy" that meets with general approbation is so conventional that it actually interferes with critical thinking. The social and literary critic R. P. Blackmur (1955, p. 16) spoke to this issue when he described what others were calling literacy as "the new illiteracy"—that is, the minimum amount of reading and writing skill for a trained population to be effectively controlled: "Ignorance is a permanently urgent problem in any society. The new illiteracy is the form that ignorance takes in societies subject to universal education." The public schools have never been eager to support students who decide to question authority, to challenge the religious and sexual patterns of their parents, to undertake much creative thinking and writing, to read a variety of political views so that they can evaluate political statements themselves. Today, in many communities, even the teaching of archeology and biology severely strains the social fabric, and standard reading (such as *Romeo and Juliet* or *Huckleberry Finn*) leads to censorship battles.

The schools, to be sure, in all societies, have an overriding social goal: to "sivilize" (as Huck Finn saw it) students into accepting their society and their place within it. Schools are in large part devoted to normalizing creative thinkers and troublemakers, training workers to accomplish efficiently what they are told to do, making things go smoothly. Training students to think independently has always been a difficult and dangerously unpopular enterprise (as Socrates could attest). In this context, it is no surprise that the mind-stunning teaching of so-called grammar and mechanics often replaces writing instruction in the schools.

Those of us in higher education might be willing to smile grimly from a distance at this description of the social imperatives that restrain the teaching of writing in the schools, but we probably would be less ready to place higher education in the same circumstances. Yet a significant portion of American higher education defines itself in similar ways, and an even larger portion of the student body sees its goals only as harmonizing with (rather than examining) the values and practices of the society. Those who contend that higher education must serve democratic political purposes as well as conforming social ones, those who argue that the coming "information society" will require a much larger number of independent thinkers than we now prepare, and those who support the goals set out in the reports alluded to in the opening pages of this book are (as they have always been to some extent) swimming upstream against a heavy current.

Whenever we look closely at what we are doing when we teach writing, we need to face the social and political implications of our decisions. Pat Bizzell (1987, p. 581), discussing some books on writing assessment, puts the issue in stark terms: "The focus on writers' knowledge demonstrates that one never learns simply 'how to write.' Rather, one learns how to write particular kinds of texts, for particular audiences, in particular languages that may be greatly removed from one's native tongue. And who learns what writing? Who has access to particular texts, audiences, languages? Since these questions are answered socially, in terms, for example, of who attends what school, the answers are subject to the political forces that shape society. Hence the 'ideology of writing' that designates some writing as 'good' and some as 'bad' tends to parallel the social ideologies that designate some ethnic, gender, and social-class groups as good, right, powerful, and others as bad, wrong, powerless. The powerful write well—by definition." Although some faculty and administrators may demur at the covert revolutionary tenor of this statement, we cannot deny that the way we teach and judge the writing of our students embodies our assumptions about society and politics.

Bizzell speaks directly to the political issue every teacher must confront in relation to student dialect variation. As we enforce the school dialect in our writing classes (as we must), we are further advantaging those whose childhood homes used this dialect—that is, the already advantaged. Some writing teachers, working within an undergraduate curriculum whose political and economic assumptions may also favor the more advantaged, find themselves uncomfortable when alert students challenge the political nature of their linguistic attitudes. But, although we should always be alert to the assumptions we are making about language, we need not feel uncomfortable as we recognize the political and social nature of our work. We are charged with inducting students into the educated community, which means, in large part, teaching them to use the school dialect effectively. We only go awry if we mistake mastery of the school dialect for intellectual ability, rather than an acquired social characteristic that is most easily accessible to the privileged.

But there is a second sense in which the teaching of writing is profoundly political. The very reading, and certainly the writing, of a poem is a political act, an assertion of individual rights, as despots have made plain; and the items on one's reading list (does American literature include Native American literature?) proclaim one's view of society. An undergraduate curriculum is a political and social as well as an educational statement. Indeed, the foundations of American education are based on a distinctly political agenda, emerging as they do from such thinkers as Thomas Jefferson, who saw public education as essential for a functioning democracy. Since democratic theory derives all power from the people, and only grants power to government with the consent of the governed, an educated populace is required; an uninformed consent is no consent at all. This political theory puts a premium on education defined as thinking and judging for oneself, and it leads directly to the kinds of statements about the function of writing that I cite in the first chapter of this book.

But, as Bizzell points out, much of education is not really concerned with stimulating individual thought and furthering democratic political concepts. Nor are most of our students particularly interested in such matters. While writing teachers may and usually do welcome original ideas, we are rather less hospitable to original spelling and punctuation—mainly because, as part of the political and social structure that Bizzell implicitly condemns, we owe it to our students to help them acquire the "right" language, the language of the rich and powerful. If we neglect that task, even in the name of equality, our students will rebel, for they are seeking the linguistic tools that will help them fit into and advance within, not challenge, the social structure. We can—and should—also help them examine and question the social structure, but no teacher working within a writing program can be separate from the socializing institution. Thus, even the most politically and socially aware writing teachers are always forced to socialize their students, even as they urge them to become more fully themselves through their writing.

English teachers delude themselves when they argue, as many do, that they are not bringing political or social issues into their classrooms. Such a delusion actually makes one more, not less, political. A teacher who is insensitive to the social and political role of dialect is likely to tell or suggest to a student that her many "mistakes in English" are the result of ignorance, derived from an uneducated home, for example. A more politically aware teacher is likely to tell such a student that the home dialect is perfectly fine in its context but will not lead to success in the school context; students who want to succeed in school have to learn the language of the school. In both cases, the teacher is upholding standards, but only the second teacher will be able to teach effectively by maintaining the self-esteem of a socially disadvantaged student. We must understand our function within the social structure of our institution, even as we know that socialization is not the most important part of our jobs. Only then can we turn our attention to the thinking skills that are central to the teaching of writing.

The problem of determining what should be taught in a writing course reflects the social and political problems I have been discussing, but the solutions must emerge in an intensely practical context. Many teachers and some WPAs become so caught up in the exhausting work of teaching writing that they have little time to consider the political implications of what they are doing, nor do they always keep in mind that the writing course has an essential role to play in the undergraduate curriculum. The following discussion of classroom procedure seeks to deal with some of the problems of teaching composition classes within those contexts.

Contents of the Writing Course

There is no professional consensus on the curriculum of writing courses, at any level. There is also no shortage of advice from researchers and practitioners; whatever approach to instruction an individual instructor might elect or inherit seems to have its prominent exemplars and promoters, and the profusion of textbooks is legendary. How can we arrange a sensible and useful syllabus in the face of so many theories, texts, research findings, pedagogical truisms, content suggestions, and methodologies? The overabundance of advice and materials sometimes seems overwhelming even to the specialists and is often beyond comprehension to the novices who are commonly entrusted with writing classes in universities.

Until more agreement emerges, if it ever does, writing teachers need to follow just a few commonsense guidelines that follow from conceiving the writing class as a critical thinking course fundamental to the liberal arts curriculum. Some of them I will look at in detail in a moment: focus on writing in the class, maintain an appropriate intellectual content, plan for discovery and revision, organize a series of writing tasks that relate to each other and call for a broad range of writing and reading skills. An outsider to the field might regard that list as so obvious that it is scarcely worth enumerating. Nonetheless, if it were to be followed, it would lead to an astounding revolution in the teaching of writing.

Whatever curriculum design emerges from consideration of the students and goals of the particular course should focus on writing tasks that *matter*, that engage our students' natural desire to make connections between their lives and their courses, to make sense of what they are learning. One way to develop assignments that matter is to make some contact with the students' lives and then to put the issue raised into a larger context. One sociologist teaching a course called "Writing in the Social Sciences" based his course on "the city." He asked his urban students to read not only Jane Jacobs but also Plato and George Orwell. He put on reserve at the library a famous laboratory report describing the effects of overcrowding on the social behavior of rats. He asked history majors in the class to come up with appropriate readings from the early Renaissance to illustrate or confute Thomas Hobbes's ideas about man in the state of nature. After intensive discussion of these materials, he posed a writing topic. What, he asked, are the legal, moral, religious, and social perspectives to bring to the murder trial of Bernard Goetz, the man who shot four threatening teenagers on a New York subway train? Meanwhile, the lone English major in the class was preparing a report to the class on Shakespeare's *As You Like It*, with its country/court division and its particular version of the pastoral.

This kind of intellectual vitality and creativity leads to good writing. Such writing, at all levels, is never neutral, voiceless, wholly detached; sometimes it even verges on personal expression and personal experience, a form of writing that is out of favor in high school and almost extinct at the college level beyond the early weeks of freshman composition courses. James Britton and his research team (1975) found very little of such important writing in the London secondary schools; many college faculty feel that it is somehow undignified to ask students to write about themselves in relation to events or ideas. But the very essence of learning is the putting of oneself in relation to the material under study. I am not advocating the intellectual aridity of unsupported personal opinion or unreflective narratives about one's own past. Too much writing in college remedial (even freshman) courses stays only with narrative, concrete descriptions, the day's news. Such a limitation essentially restricts student possibilities for learning and for an expanded context for thought (Ohmann, 1979). But a course that draws on and helps to integrate the general education program, a course that asks students to evaluate what they read and say, leads to the critical thinking that can generate writing worth writing and reading.

A college-level writing course, then, treads a narrow curricular line, whatever the material it uses or the approach it takes. It needs to help students place themselves in contact with their topics, using some kind of appropriate voice, even as it asks them as writers to discover and develop ideas found in reading and discussion beyond themselves. The class needs to attend to the machinery of writing, from punctuation and spelling to audience awareness, but only in passing and as appropriate to the real focus of the course: inventing, reading, critical thinking, drafting, and revising. Further, the reading and the writing assignments need to relate to each other and to move in some discernible way from the beginning of the term to the end.

Too many undergraduate writing courses and writing programs show inattention to these commonsense matters. On many campuses, students placed in a "remedial" curriculum are asked to complete grammar workbooks or a series of writing assignments that avoid abstractions and complex reading. Many freshman composition programs have little or no reading as well. Often, the writing assignments seem so self-contained that they do not connect with each other, or with the rest of the general education program.

Nor does new technology help with curriculum. Despite the enthusiasm of new computer users, the promise that word processing will lead to better writing (as opposed to more writing) has not yet been fulfilled. In recent years, computer word processing and editing programs have been replacing the rote drill-and-practice uses to which computers were put when they first became available; however, so much time may be taken up in developing computer literacy that writing instruction can be left behind, and meaningful reading may simply disappear. Even the promise that ease of revision by computer will lead to more and better revision has not yet been kept; students must want to revise, and must learn what and how to revise, before the computers will help them much.

Since the definition of writing instruction is so inclusive, and since there is no professional agreement on the best way to approach the teaching of writing, the curriculum can easily go awry. I have been speaking of the problem of a writing curriculum bereft of intellectual substance, but the substitution of disciplinary material for writing is no answer. Sometimes, in an effort to make the writing course substantial, a teacher will allow engaging literature or unengaging linguistic material to become the real focus for the course. It is not always easy to say when the substitution has taken place, since most writing teachers will use some grammatical terminology and some reading. As we consider the writing curriculum, and its need for an emphasis on critical thinking, we must resist even well-intentioned attempts to change the writing course into something else. There is also a serious truth-in-packaging argument here, one to which higher education is vulnerable. Despite the beliefs of some faculty members, they do not have the right to change the course curriculum approved by curriculum committees, faculty senates, and university administrations. The college catalogue is a kind of contract with students, in many institutions actually a legal contract, and students sitting in a composition course have the right to expect the composition course described in that catalogue. It is neither a violation of academic freedom nor inappropriate snooping for the WPA to ensure that courses in that program are designed to achieve their stated goals. It is dishonest, perhaps illegal, to substitute a different kind of course for one called composition, whatever the motive may be.

Keeping the Focus on Writing

My youngest son's high school freshman composition class was typical of a certain kind of commonly misplaced instruction. He spent the entire year memorizing grammatical terminology and filling in workbooks. He became expert at correcting errors in the workbooks, though he routinely committed those same errors in his own prose (in letters to family and friends—the only writing he performed that year). He neither wrote a word of his own nor read a page of anything except workbook material in this misnamed class. In short, he had the kind of instructional focus that Hillocks described (see Chapter Three) as the least effective option.

During the school open house, I questioned the teacher about the absence of writing. "In *my* class," he declaimed, "students learn the basics. Then they are ready to write in other classes." When I asked him why he imagined workbook grammar to be the "basics," he looked at me as if I were mad. "How can they write if they don't know the parts of speech?" he said. Despite the teacher's ignorance—or because of it—my son rather enjoyed the year, since he caught on to the game fairly quickly and could solve the word problems without much thought; at thirteen, he liked the idea that language was governed by simple rules with clear right and wrong answers. Best of all, there was no writing to do, despite the title of the course.

Although my son learned almost nothing useful (and what he did learn was largely wrong), he received a good grade and felt rewarded. The teacher, though he did more harm than good, felt ennobled by his labor, which, he was convinced, embodied high standards and classical virtues. Unlike some less structured teachers, whose students wrote unpredictable kinds of things or whose classes were noisy, he always knew exactly what he was teaching, and he could demonstrate through multiple-choice tests just how well his students were doing.

Such teachers are absolutely convinced of the value of what they ask their students to do and are in no way influenced by argument or by research to change their ways. They can be found not only in the public schools but everywhere in educational institutions, and they often dominate remedial or even freshman composition programs at the college level. I have encountered numbers of them in upper-division writing-across-the-curriculum programs; their doctorates may be in anthropology or chemistry, but they somehow feel it necessary to teach what they believe to be grammar in their writing classes.

This connection of school grammar to the teaching of writing is not a trivial matter; it causes problems throughout the undergraduate curriculum. When we seek to enhance the campus climate for writing by building writing courses into departmental offerings, we frequently run into troubling resistance from literate and concerned faculty in various fields of study. Sometimes these faculty are well aware of the importance of writing to learning in their own fields and are highly supportive of English department writing courses. But they will neither teach nor support the teaching of writing courses outside of English; if writing winds up in their department course schedule, they will seek out English faculty or English graduate students to do the teaching. This paradoxical behavior, I am convinced, stems from a deeply embedded identification of writing with school grammar. Since these faculty don't know grammar, as they will freely admit, they feel disqualified from teaching writing or, particularly, from responding to student writing. No matter what the facts may be, they believe that those in English are specialists in writing because they know grammar. Before we can see writing as an effective part of the undergraduate curriculum, we must find ways to free these teachers from this identification of grammar with writing instruction. Unhappily, enough writing teachers reinforce the belief to make refutation difficult.

One of the great puzzles of American education is the persistence of this kind of instruction, despite the accumulated evidence of its ineffectiveness. If we are to understand why the teaching of writing by means of "grammar" continues and flourishes, and how we may combat it, we need to examine a few of the principal arguments that support it.

1. "Students need to know grammar in order to write." Two different definitions of "knowing grammar" are at work in this familiar sentence: an ability to use the underlying rules of the language and an ability to identify and name these abstract rules according to some grammatical system. The assumption here is that humans first learn abstract theory and then go on to actual practice. A little reflection shows that most human learning proceeds differently: abstractions follow rather than precede concrete experience. There is also an important difference between the kind of knowledge people acquire as they learn language naturally and the knowledge of formal grammatical terminology or systems that is taught in school. Linguists claim that native speakers "know" (that is, can use effectively) the grammar of their language by the age of five or six; only a few specialists in linguistics need learn the enormously complicated grammatical rules and terminology of English. Most teachers seriously underestimate the complexity of formal grammar, which is a description of the way a language in fact behaves; few teachers (or writers, for that matter) have or need much systematic and abstract understanding of English grammar, one of the most complex in the world.

Of course, one of the problems all teachers face is ungrammatical student writing. Naive teachers, encountering confusion of verb tenses, or reference, or agreement, or sentence structure, assume that they can correct the situation by teaching school grammar. They are supported in this assumption by the students, who often themselves believe that an additional dose of grammar will make them better writers. A more logical supporting argument is that some common grammatical terminology (such as "subject" and "verb") in fact does make it easier to talk with students about their writing, though some experienced writing teachers will let even this terminology arise contextually, so that it can be "owned" by the students.

But there are two overwhelming reasons for avoiding the teaching of grammar in place of writing instruction: (1) the students already *know* how to use the grammar of their native language, and drilling them in the naming of what they know does not help them use what they know; and (2) for twenty-five years, research studies have consistently demonstrated that formal grammar instruction does not help students write better.

One of the great frustrations of teaching writing is that students do not use what they already know. Some canny teachers ask freshmen to read aloud in conference what they have submitted in writing and to correct the work as they read. Most freshmen seem able to correct the errors that bother the teacher. Just as they can do well on multiple-choice tests of error recognition, they can, when asked, recognize their own errors. But they continue to make them. It also seems clear to many experienced teachers that students make fewer errors after they gain more interest in what they write, more stake in what they say, more investment in writing as a thinking and discovering (rather than an error-avoiding) activity. The teacher's problem, then, is not to learn how to teach yet more grammar but to understand why some students care so little, and think so little, about what they are writing that they continue to make the same familiar, damaging errors. Every teacher also needs to know the difference between grammatical error and dialectal variation.

The research on grammar and the teaching of writing is the clearest in the field. In the first authoritative review of research in composition, the single most resounding sentence had to do with grammar: "In view of the widespread agreement of research studies based upon many types of students and teachers, the conclusion can be stated in strong and unqualified terms: the teaching of formal grammar has a negligible or, because it usually displaces some instruction and practice in actual composition, even a harmful effect on the improvement of writing"

(Braddock, Lloyd-Jones, and Schoer, 1963, pp. 37–38). As we have seen, George Hillocks, reviewing another generation of research, says much the same thing (1986, pp. 133–151). Hillocks sees some useful possibilities for instruction in near-grammar work, such as sentence combining, but is unable to find gains in composition ability or even in correctness in writing (as opposed to performance on multiple-choice tests) from any existing grammar exercises. The evidence does not dispute the value of correct writing, but it does show that the direct teaching of correctness fails to reach that goal.

2. "The students keep asking me to teach grammar and punctuation." Every experienced writing teacher has learned to turn aside such earnest requests from students, since the pleas are based on a pervasive student mythology about writing and writing instruction. That is, college students, in their heart of hearts, believe that a handful of rules (which can be learned through drill) will transform ordinary students into good writers. They, of course, don't know what these rules are, but English teachers are supposed to have the inside information and they aren't telling. If students could only learn these rules, they believe, they could then turn out perfect first drafts, which they believe good writers invariably do. In fact, every student has picked up and clings to one or two of these rules: never use the word "I," avoid all contractions, use lots of Latin terms such as "ibid," always use the comma after the name of a tree, and so on. The fact that the supposed rules are wrong or ridiculous in no way diminishes the fervor with which they are held. Furthermore, the students imagine that Miss Grundy handed out these rules in the fifth grade on the day they were sick; thus, everyone else *does* know all the rules, a belief fraught with a subjective sense of frustrated inferiority in the face of now inaccessible knowledge.

The student demand for more "grammar," then, when it is not a cynical way to avoid the real work of a writing course, is the result of a consistently taught misunderstanding of what writing consists of. The assumptions behind this request need to be brought out into the open through discussion, as part of the writing class itself. Since learning centers and tutors (not to speak of many computer programs) are on hand to help with spelling and the like, college faculty members should not allow themselves to be persuaded to waste class time on material that is as useless as it is familiar to students.

Maintaining an Appropriate Intellectual Content in Composition

Partly in reaction to the emptiness and uselessness of the grammar curriculum for composition, composition faculty with training in other fields (and almost all college composition teachers have received advanced degrees in some field other than writing) are tempted to substitute the content of those fields for writing instruction, particularly when they think that writing instruction means the mysteries of grammar. Those responsible for composition programs are thus often confronted with a very practical question: When is a subject matter (such as literature or the city) *supporting* the teaching of composition and when is it *substituting for* the teaching of composition? How can we be sure to maintain sufficient intellectual content in the writing curriculum without allowing subject matter to replace writing?

I do not agree with certain specialists in composition who maintain that any outside content is a distraction in the writing course. I value writing about the self and also writing about the self in relation to others or to the expression of others. But, as I have asserted in various ways in this book, college composition also calls for serious and careful inquiry, discovery, and development of thought beyond the self. Such thought must be about *something* outside the self and hence involves reading—that is, some subject matter. Sometimes the purists in composition instruction remind me of the novelist Mary McCarthy's cruel Uncle Myers and Aunt Mary; the theory behind their tyranny over the McCarthy orphans, she later wrote in *Memories of a Catholic Girlhood*, was "to achieve efficiency": "our lives, in order to be open, had to be empty" (1957, p. 71). College composition courses ought not to "be empty" of intellectual challenge in order to avoid distraction from attractive subject matter.

If we accept or endorse (as I do) the value of serious concepts and reading within the composition course, we need to use other criteria to determine whether we still have a writing course. The problem is, however, more difficult in theory than it turns out to be in practice. When substitution is involved, the writing becomes incidental to the real subject; when we have a writing course, the content becomes incidental to the student writing and rewriting. Some questions become obvious: What proportion of class time is spent in such activities as prewriting, journal writing, evaluating drafts, small-group peer discussion of student writing, teacher-led discussion of sample student papers, and the like? Does the material allow reasonable scope for a variety of student interests, for a series of writing assignments with a coherent purpose related to increasing student writing skill, for revision and development of student ideas? Does the syllabus and the grading machinery allow time for and reward revision of writing, and is student writing ability the main criterion for the final grade? Are student-teacher conferences about writing built into the course plan?

Or, on the other hand, is the course built around mastery of the content: Do the classes, the tests, the design of the course follow the usual pattern of other kinds of courses, whose appropriate goal is understanding of a body of material and concepts? Is the only student writing a "product," such as a term paper, that is largely the student's responsibility and is handed in at the end of the course? Are most classes devoted to lectures on or discussion of the reading? Is the course grade wholly or largely dependent on tests and other measures of mastery of content?

For example, the usual, and entirely appropriate, Shakespeare class will define a group of a dozen or more plays by date ("early") or by kind ("tragedies") or the like. The students will spend their time reading the plays, perhaps writing an occasional limited short paper on one of them (say, the meaning of suicide in *Hamlet* or the clothing imagery in *Lear*), and probably writing a term paper on some aspect of the plays read or on some topic relating the plays to the English Renaissance. The students may read some Shakespeare criticism, see videos or live perfor-

mances, or undertake other activities to deepen their understanding of Shakespeare. There will be a final examination, and
perhaps a mid-term as well, to evaluate the depth of their
knowledge.

Such a course should not be called a writing class, even
though it may include a good bit of student writing. The writing
is there to support the learning and understanding of Shakespeare
(as it should), and writing instruction is incidental to the major
goal of the course. Some readers will remember the widespread
attacks on required composition courses during the 1960s,
when curriculum committees and the faculty as a whole became
unwilling to accept such literature courses as writing courses.
Why should these courses meet writing requirements merely because they were taught by the English department, when they
were no more aimed at teaching writing than well-conceived
courses in many other departments were? English departments
had few convincing arguments beyond pointing to the innate
value of literature and the tradition of departmental concern for
improving student writing. University curriculum committees
responded by recommending that the literature requirements be
maintained and (on many campuses) that the writing requirement be cut back or eliminated. A few campuses simply set up a
composition department separate from the English department,
a development I deplored at some length in Chapter Three.

It is not hard, however, to conceive of a writing course
based on Shakespeare (or any other content area). Such a course
would use the plays to provide content for a variety of writing
assignments. Perhaps one sequence could move from a description of a performance to a review of the performance to a research paper on classic performances of the same play. A comparison of *Much Ado About Nothing* and *Othello* (with their
similar story lines) could lead to a series of papers comparing
comedy with tragedy as artistic forms or even as approaches to
understanding experience. Class time would be spent largely on
the writing problems posed by the course—though, naturally
enough, some attention would be given to the reading of the
plays. But now the understanding of Shakespeare would be an-
cillary to the student writing, and the students' grades would

depend much more on their writing than on the depth of their
understanding of the plays within the Renaissance context.

Planning Assignments for Discovery and Revision

Writing courses should undermine the student attitude
that is embodied in the night-before all-night typing orgy which
is the normal means of production for most student essays, whatever the level or subject.

Most teachers carry over into their own instruction the
patterns of writing assignments that were current in the classes
they took as students. Sometime around the middle of the term,
students received a general term paper assignment, often clear
only in the number of pages or sources required; the paper was
due at the end of the term; the teacher functioned as judge of
performance, grading the paper with (perhaps) a brief comment
added: "*A—* very good." If students wished, they could confer
with the professor in advance about the paper, but relatively
few did; since the paper was to be written the night before it
was due, there really wasn't very much to talk about. And there
was no point in talking about the paper after it was graded, since
the term was over and they had new courses to deal with. Some
unscrupulous students would purchase a paper to hand in from
"research services" or copy one from fraternity files, and these
papers often received excellent grades. No one ever imagined
that more than one draft should be produced. At most, an initial draft would be retyped with an eye to neatness, spelling,
and footnote format, the principal criteria for good grades according to folk lore (and much experience). I wish I could say
that this pattern no longer held true.

Writing-across-the-curriculum programs universally seek
to help faculty develop more useful patterns for students. But
few of us who direct such programs have found successful ways
to overcome resistance to change in this area; the term paper in
its traditional form seems even more deeply embedded in most
college faculty than is the teaching of "grammar." Even when
we turn to the curriculum of the composition course, we often
see signs of the same syndrome—unsurprisingly, since few fac-

ulty have received any training in the teaching of writing. It should be a firm underlying principle of any writing course that revision is central to the writing process. Teachers who function simply as judges of writing products are not teaching writing. The grading of papers is not, in fact, the same thing as the teaching of writing.

Since virtually all professional writers spend substantial amounts of time revising their work, a useful writing course will profit from this experience and seek to establish new patterns that emphasize revision. Experienced composition faculty are likely to use some or all of the following ways to include revision as part of the class.

1. *Writing Assignments Presented in Written Form.* The first step in eliciting good writing from students is the distribution of a written assignment to the students. Many teachers fail to hand out such an assignment, simply telling the students what they want or jotting something on the chalk board to be (more or less) copied. Such casual treatment of the assignment suggests that a similarly casual response is called for. Even a written and discussed assignment often leads to misunderstandings by the students; less careful assignments routinely lead to confusion. "Oh," the student will say, "I didn't remember what you wanted [when I wrote the essay the night before it was due]." Experienced teachers have usually learned that they must write out their assignments if they are to be taken seriously, but newer teachers are constantly being surprised at the range of misunderstandings that occur despite their painstaking oral explanations.

Some teachers prefer to let students choose their own subjects for writing, on the grounds that such openness will encourage creativity and a greater sense of ownership of the topic. With undefined topics, however, a large part of the energy available for writing must go into selecting and defining and redefining a topic; if more than one or two such exercises are included in the writing course, students have less opportunity than they should have to learn other aspects of the writing process, such as development and demonstration of ideas, use of sources, and revision. Open topics, in my experience, are more likely to signify an unclear course design than a commitment to independent and creative thought; such topics are also an open invitation to the unscrupulous to purchase their essays from the supplies available on and off campus.

Despite these problems, some superior writing teachers remain committed to open assignments; they are convinced that students will write better when they are free to choose what they will write about. These teachers must make extra efforts to overcome the problems I have been describing. Their students must receive a description of the purpose of the assignment, its format, and the criteria that will be used in evaluating it. Much class time has to be spent discussing topics and helping students define, limit, and focus what they expect to say. Class time alone is insufficient for many students, who will need individual attention during (and after) office hours. During the writing process, the students should be required to submit plans, outlines, drafts, bibliographies, and the like, because the open assignment requires careful attention to the writing process and the development of a common set of standards, and the frequent submissions ensure that the student is actually doing the work. No doubt, this system helps students write more effectively. But this elaborate and labor-intensive pedagogy is not what we often see; open assignments are more often a symptom of lack of time than a commitment to intensive extra time with individual students.

Erika Lindemann, in a fine book for writing teachers, has suggested a series of questions for faculty to ask themselves about their writing assignments; the following version of that "heuristic" (adapted from Lindemann, 1982, pp. 208–209) suggests the kind of thinking that ought to go into the making of assignments that can support constructive writing instruction.

1. *What do I want the students to do?* Is it worth doing? Why? Is it interesting and appropriate? What will it teach the students? Specifically? How does it fit my objectives at this point in the course? What will the assignment tell me? What is being assessed? Does the task have meaning outside as well as inside the class setting? Have I given enough class time to discussion of these goals?
2. *How do I want the students to do the assignment?* Are stu-

dents working alone or together? In what ways will they practice prewriting, writing, revising? Have I given enough information about what I want so students can make effective choices about subject, purpose, form, mode, and tone? Have I given enough information about required length and about the use of sources? Have I prepared and distributed a written assignment with clear directions? Are good examples appropriate? Have I given enough class time to discussion of these procedures?

3. *For whom are the students writing?* Who is the audience? If the audience is the teacher, do the students know enough about this teacher's particular expectations so that they can make the appropriate assumptions and take the appropriate tone? Are there ways and reasons to expand the audience beyond the teacher? Have I given enough class time to discussion of audience?

4. *When will students do the assignment?* How does the assignment relate to what comes before and after it in the course? Is the assignment sequenced to give enough time for prewriting, writing, revision, and editing? How much time in and outside of class will students need? To what extent will I guide and grade the students' work? What deadlines (and penalties) do I want to set for collecting papers, or various stages of the project? Have I given enough class time to discussion of the writing process?

5. *What will I do with the assignment?* How will I evaluate the work? What constitutes a successful response to the assignment? Will other students or the writer have a say in evaluating the paper? Does the grading system encourage revision? Have I attempted to write the paper myself? What problems did I encounter? How can the assignment be clarified or otherwise improved? Have I discussed evaluation criteria with the students?

The questions in point 4 speak directly to a deadline schedule for submission of stages of the work. Depending on the assignment, this schedule could call for notes, bibliographies, abstracts, plans, outlines, sections, drafts, or whatever is most appropriate. A simple deadline schedule for each assignment has two important benefits: (1) it enforces the need for the student to get going quickly and to work steadily at the task, instead of trying to handle the assignment the night before the final due date; and (2) it largely defeats plagiarism, since early stages of the bought or borrowed paper are unlikely to be available.

The written assignment must be discussed carefully with the students. For example, since a deadline for plans or drafts is foreign to most students' experience, they probably will ignore it unless it is explained in detail. To illustrate just what the task calls for, teachers can hand out duplicated scoring guides (or develop one with the class) and samples of successful previous papers. If enough time is allowed for discussion of the assignment, students will leave the class session with an understanding of what is required, and why, and also of various possible ways to approach the job. And they will know that a last-minute first draft will not fulfill the task. A good assignment will always reinforce the need to draft and revise drafts and will distinguish the cognitive work of revision from the editorial work of correcting errors.

The construction of appropriate writing assignments is one of the hardest jobs for the teacher of undergraduates, probably rendered harder than it needs to be by the dearth of supportive material available. (For a fuller discussion of this issue, see White, 1985, pp. 100–119.) Every teacher should keep in mind that the writing of assignments is a particularly demanding form of *writing*, calling for the entire writing process, most particularly revision.

2. *Prewriting.* Students will write better if they are required to think systematically before they put pen to paper. Although scholars debate about the most effective kind of prewriting, there is a clear consensus that active engagement with the assignment before the start of writing is immensely valuable; prewriting not only improves the quality of the work to be done but also trains students to use a crucial part of the writing process. (See Witte, 1987a, for recent research and careful discussion of this concept.) Some composition faculty use formal methods derived from logic or problem solving (sometimes called

heuristics); other teachers use various forms of brainstorming, cognitive mapping, or clustering of ideas. Still others ask students to do unstructured "five-minute writes" or free writing or aptly named "discovery drafts" as ways to uncover or develop ideas. These are all forms of what classical rhetoric called "invention": the finding of topics for development. The very word *topic* comes from the Greek word for "place," suggesting that the thinking process is a kind of geographical quest, a hunt for a place where ideas lurk.

Any assignment worth doing is worth discussing. The most valuable discussion often emerges from presentation of what the other students in the class are working on. As students hear what their peers are planning to do, they begin to envision new possibilities. And when they express their own thoughts on the subject, they begin to acquire ownership of their topic. Moreover, early notes and reading give them an unaccustomed start toward more satisfying writing than their previous training and habits have led them to expect.

3. *Teaching and Grading Invention and Revision.* We may talk about writing as discovery and revision, and even schedule due dates for work in progress; but unless we build respect for revision into our evaluation of writing, our students will not believe us. If we continue to give a single grade for the finished (or not-so-finished) writing product, we are in fact saying that the product is all that we value. Thus, the argument for rewarding the work in progress (through grades) is compelling, and not only for the reasons I have been stating. Term papers, and student essays in general, are among the least valuable products in a world of waste paper; only a tiny percentage of them are saved, and only a minuscule percentage are published. True, they serve as products to be graded; but the only real reason for their production is as testimony to student learning. In many cases, that learning is better measured through the steps of production than through only the final formal product.

This is a delicate balance. Some teachers handle it by giving grades on one kind of scale for drafts, bibliographies, and the like—say, a numerical scale similar to that used in many holistic scoring sessions (typically, "6" high to "1" low). The final draft then can be graded on the usual A to F scale. It all depends on the goals of the course and the assignment. But the central point remains: Any composition instruction that attempts to instill good writing habits will both require and grade stages of the discovery and revision process.

We need to be careful about our real messages in this regard. Unfortunately, numbers of well-meaning writing instructors include revision in their course plans either as an unpleasant option or as punishment for bad work. Sometimes papers graded below B may or must be revised; sometimes revision is a possibility only if the students wish to raise their grades. In a great many classes, revision means merely editing for mechanics or making only the teacher's proposed changes. But every real writer knows that revision means a new "vision" of what is being said, responding to internal, not external, demands; *every* piece of writing in a writing class should be revised as a matter of normal routine, as a part of the thinking process that writing expresses.

4. *Authority, Responsibility, and Ownership.* One major difference between the teaching of writing and the teaching of other subject matter has to do with the role of the teacher. In most college courses, the teacher maintains authority (through expertness in the field), is responsible for the substance of what students are to learn, and maintains ownership of the course. However, each of these concepts operates differently in the writing course.

The teacher, of course, continues to exercise the authority that derives from knowledge and experience. In most cases, the teacher knows more about writing than the students do, has done more writing than the students have, and is a more practiced and skillful reader than the students are. Therefore, the teacher has the authority to structure the syllabus, make assignments, and evaluate student writing. But the students will not learn much about writing if they are merely passive recipients of the teacher's knowledge. The studies by Hillocks, summarized in Chapter Three, support the need for active participation by students in the writing class if effective learning is to take place. Since the students must think their own thoughts, invent, discover, write, and revise, they must themselves develop some kind of authority; no one can write very well unless he or she has something to say, which implies a certain kind of authority over the material.

Thus, the teacher must be willing to share some of the authority that adheres to the instructor's role. If they are to write with a real voice, students must believe that they have, or can gain, authority over their material. When they write about personal experience, that authority usually comes naturally enough; they are the only ones who really know what happened, and they have the right to speculate on what it means. But that tenuous sense of authority tends to disappear in the face of analytical assignments or printed sources. Frequently, students will only describe something that the assignment asks them to evaluate; or they will simply summarize or quote someone's argument, even though the assignment asks them to relate it to their own (or someone else's) ideas. Adolescent assertiveness about everything has in college yielded to a trained unwillingness to take a stand or claim authority before the "expert" professor or the printed source. Therefore, the writing teacher must find ways to help students understand the kind of authority all writers can claim (or earn). Some students simply cannot write for professors who assert, or seem to claim, too much authority over too many aspects of the material. Young and relatively insecure teachers, I suspect, are particularly prone to this attitude; I know that I was. I remember well a student's hesitant question after I gave the class an assignment to write about a Renaissance poet: "Are we supposed to like Skelton?" Like many good students, she had given all authorial authority (note the relation of the two words) to the teacher, or, more likely, I had unwittingly laid claim to so much authority that she saw no space to assert any of her own.

Many conscientious writing teachers not only deprive their students of the authority all writers need but also unintentionally assume responsibility for the papers their students produce. The most obvious sign of this shifting of responsibility from the student to the teacher occurs when the student tries to revise an early draft in the light of the teacher's comments. Almost invariably, the student will not change anything that the teacher left alone; all revisions focus on the corrections suggested by the teacher. The result is often very odd, sometimes considerably worse than the original. The revised portions of the paper are often much better, particularly if the teacher's comments led the student to rethink and reorganize her best ideas (as comments should). But the paper as a whole is now out of balance, with the original untouched portions, which seemed all right in the draft, now much in need of work. When we say this, the student is often outraged: "You saw nothing wrong with it before!" In the student's eyes, and perhaps in our own, we have become responsible for some, or all, of the paper. "Is this what you wanted?" we may hear, as if it were now *our* paper.

The attitude we take in our comments is crucial here. We need to convey to the student writer that responsibility and ownership remain with him (see Sommers, 1982). We ought not to assume the role of editor for the student (marking every error is a common mistake, leading to student frustration or apathy in the face of too much red ink), nor ought we to tell the student what the paper should do. We should rather assert our problems with the paper, if we have them, and ask the writer to try to resolve these problems. At most, we might suggest some options or alternatives, but we must refrain from taking over the paper—even if we are convinced that we know just what it ought to be doing. Pointed questions are often more effective than assertions: "This seems to be your central idea; why does it first appear here, in the next-to-last paragraph?" "The second half of this paper seems to be on a different topic than the first half; which topic do you want to focus on?" (See Walvoord, 1986, for many practical and helpful ideas about commenting on student papers.)

A sensible posture to take toward drafts is to comment only on a few central matters: the ideas, the structure, the author's perspective or voice, for example. Certainly, sound pedagogy suggests that all comments contain something positive. Perhaps a comment about mechanics at the end ("The paper has sentence errors that ought not to appear in the final draft") might be useful in some cases. But good teaching is clear about goals; therefore, if we assume that substantial rewriting of the current draft will take place, we ought not to fuss about the spelling of words that may well disappear. We need to encourage risk taking in drafts, the trying on of ideas and arguments that may not work out or that may turn out to be very exciting. The challenge of responding to student work is not only in rendering fair judgments (more about this below) but in coaching and fostering the process.

The Unifying Power of the Writing Course

I have been speaking here about ways of organizing and teaching a writing course within the undergraduate degree program. Most colleges and universities offer such courses at several levels (perhaps all levels) of instruction, and some institutions will locate the courses outside as well as inside the English department. Still other campuses will expect certain departmental courses (perhaps those with a "W" designation) to include substantial writing components, as part of a university writing requirement. These courses are usually valuable for students, and I have been discussing some of the ways they can be made more valuable. The good teaching practices I have been recommending all relate to the writing course as a critical-thinking class centered within the liberal arts curriculum.

But in the American college curriculum, with its departmental fragmentation, writing is separated from most learning. If "English" or "expository writing" takes care of writing, then the rest of the institution is free to go about its business of teaching ever more narrowly defined subjects. Most reports assessing the undergraduate curriculum mention the lack of unity or even a lack of relationship among the discrete parts. What is often called general education turns out on most campuses to be a series of elementary courses in the disciplines, with the student expected to integrate these courses so that they form a cohesive pattern. The college graduate has met major requirements, general education requirements, and elective requirements, usually through a series of discrete courses. Behind this curriculum lies an epistemology: knowledge and learning are taken to be accumulative activities, and the accumulations are kept separate rather than combining with and reinforcing one another. Thus, one writes in the English course, reasons in philosophy, calculates in mathematics, experiments in the science laboratory, and so on. Each activity is seen as equally valuable, with the same number of "credits," and no one of these subjects is allowed to gain enough power to include the others. A student who seeks to reason both philosophically and mathematically, test her ideas in the laboratory, and write the results artistically simply has nowhere to go on most university campuses. This is an epistemology that embodies political assumptions about the role of learning in society. Since a college education turns out to be an accumulation of bits and pieces, we do not expect this kind of learning to be useful beyond a narrow vocational sense.

Thus, the questions usually asked about the place of writing within the curriculum, trapped as they are within this epistemology, fail to approach the possibilities that writing has to offer. A committee may ask, "How many units of English composition courses should be required?" (On most campuses, that question would be perceived as a political and financial issue, not an educational one.) It would make more sense to try to figure out how much writing, and what kinds of writing, should be required of a student receiving the degree. Some of that writing would surely take place in English composition courses, but some of it would belong elsewhere. Campuses that require a senior thesis or a "capstone" general education writing course are using writing as a powerful integrating and unifying force. But those who continue to think of writing as one more piece of accumulated knowledge are, in effect, harnessing the power of language and thought to a production model, instead of releasing that power for creative and critical thought. This issue returns us to the political discussion at the beginning of this chapter. Writing needs to be taught both in and out of the English department—indeed, in every department in one way or another— so that students, through this active participation in their own education, can put things together. The integration of the self can combat the fragmentation of the curriculum, but that is no easy task. Nonetheless, it is this vision of writing that lies at the core of undergraduate education, promoting individual thought, considered response, intellectual creativity, and the unifying power of the mind.

Chapter 5

Defining Purposes and Issues in the Assessment of Writing Ability

Assessment is a polarizing issue in American education. On the one side are those who reasonably argue that assessment is a necessary element of all learning ("How'm I doin'?") and an appropriate way for institutions to discover their effectiveness. On the other side are those who reasonably argue that the present overemphasis on assessment distorts learning (particularly with inappropriate or invalid tests) and reduces complicated matters to those that are easily measurable. The polarization assumes large political and social dimensions as well. Those who favor assessment are often from off campus and are suspected by many faculty of association with political and economic interests intent on preserving discriminatory economic and social structures; those who oppose assessment are usually campus faculty and students who see themselves acting on behalf of the less privileged. Those in power tend to foster or demand assessment, and those who are or perceive themselves to be powerless (students, many teachers, minority groups, and the like) argue against the imposition of most testing devices.

However, the issue is far from clear-cut. In a society with limited positions of status and power, individual assessment can be one of the few routes to advancement for those not born to privilege. Thus, one could argue that tests such as the Scholastic Aptitude Test (SAT), used to award scholarships and (in part) admission to higher education, offer opportunities to the very groups that protest their use; the Educational Testing Service argues that the SAT in fact "overpredicts" college success for minorities. Without the evidence of ability provided by the test, numbers of underprivileged able students would not be able to prove their promise. But the evidence that the SAT presents of continued low group scores for some minorities leads to a series of less favorable hypotheses—for example, that the test contains subtle biases, that it merely confirms present notions of ability and persistence, that it perpetuates stereotypes. Some maintain that the test simply presents the results of social, racial, and economic discrimination in the nation and its school system, and hence provides valuable information for those seeking to promote justice and equality; others, accepting the same premise, would just as soon kill the messenger. Similar complex arguments whirl about virtually every significant assessment program in the country. All that is clear is that any simple statement is bound to be one-sided and wrong.

Colleges and their faculties tend to be caught in the middle of these arguments. In general, funding sources, political figures, and institutional administrators favor testing as an administrative convenience for admissions, placement, course equivalency, program evaluation, and (sometimes) exit proficiency; there is often an implied threat that budgetary decisions may be influenced by assessment results. The faculties are normally suspicious of the assessments favored by the administration, though they retain a relatively uncritical faith in their own. The nearer we get to real live students, the less sure we become about generalized groupings and tests designed for different populations than the one before us; the more we are involved with teaching, the less sympathetic we become to the purely administrative purposes of testing. Yet faculties are charged with unremitting evaluation of students, which they perform as well as they can, term in and term out, and institutional managers are normally uncomfortable with the ambiguous results obtained by the usual assessment instruments.

All these problems become exacerbated in the field of writing, where reliable and valid assessments have always been rare. Chapters Six and Nine detail the institutional uses of writing tests, with some of their problems and possibilities. Our concern in this chapter is with issues rather than organization or applications: in the light of current practice and research, to consider the most effective means of assessing student writing for institutional and instructional purposes—that is, to rank students for the perceived needs of the institution and to help individual students write better (see Brown, 1986; Greenberg, Wiener, and Donovan, 1986, pp. 44–52).

Whatever the purpose or uses of a writing assessment, certain polarities invariably present themselves: multiple-choice versus essay testing, norm referencing versus criterion referencing, usage or "grammar" versus thought or organization, teacher involvement versus teacher distance from testing, high cost with validity and instructional value versus cheap and handy testing without those benefits.

Multiple-Choice Versus Essay Testing

Until recently, advocates of indirect, usually multiple-choice, measurement of writing ability could point to the high cost and low reliability of scoring writing samples, as compared with the low cost and high efficiency of multiple-choice answer sheets. However, with the development of relatively reliable and cost-effective holistic procedures for the scoring of essay tests, the argument has shifted. Those opposed to multiple-choice measurement of writing can now point to the high development costs of multiple-choice testing, the constant security and revision expenses of multiple-choice tests under truth-in-testing laws, the lower validity of such tests, and the damage to writing instruction such tests cause by devaluing the activity they set out to measure.

A number of studies have sought to relate the scores students receive on multiple-choice tests with those the same students receive on a writing sample. The correlations vary somewhat, as one would expect from the great number of variables involved (different kinds of students, items, essay questions, scoring systems, and the like), but they tend to hover about the .5 range. The number, as usual, raises more questions than it answers. The correlation is roughly the same as that between an adult female's height and weight in America. That is, one can guess a woman's weight from her given height with about the same accuracy that one can guess a student's essay score from his or her multiple-choice score. Is that level of accuracy good enough? Partisans of multiple-choice testing will argue that the correlation is good enough for many decisions, such as a placement test (where misplacements can be reshuffled during the first week of classes without too much difficulty) and good enough to support the inclusion of a significant number of multiple-choice items on any writing test. They will also argue that the score on the essay test is itself not definitive (since it is also an approximation of real writing ability under artificial circumstances) and that an essay test has the disadvantage of being a "one-question" test of first-draft writing (which poses its own validity problem). Those opposed to multiple-choice testing find the correlations too low, particularly in the light of evidence that the correlation drops markedly for minority groups (White, 1985, pp. 71–83). (See also Koenig and Mitchell, 1988, for an interim report supporting the racial fairness of essay testing. The report notes that score differences by race on the pilot essay portion of the Medical College Admissions Test "were largely related to reading level.") If, as statisticians point out, a rough guide to the "overlap" of any two measures is the square of the correlation, only about 25 percent of what is measured on most writing sample tests is also measured on most multiple-choice "writing" tests.

Most writing teachers are opposed to multiple-choice testing of writing ability for many reasons beyond the statistical one, largely because such testing devalues their definition of and goals for writing. They reject the common parlance for such testing, finding it anything but "objective." When test developers call multiple-choice tests "objective," they are rendering a judgment of questionable value, not giving a description. The *scoring* of these tests is certainly objective and reliable, since it is done by machine, but the *creation* of the tests is the result of a series of subjective decisions (decisions about what constitutes writing and how that is to be measured). Since these decisions are rarely made by writers or even by writing teachers, the intensely subjective and (often) linguistically naive nature of the supposedly objective tests is all too evident. Writers and writing teachers are not bothered by what test specialists call the "one-question" essay test, because they know that the writing act combines a large number of skills of all sorts. (Nonetheless, it is noticeably more fair to students to require more than one writing sample on an important essay test.) When the multiple-choice test attempts to break these skills into machine-scorable and separate parts, it changes their nature—just as the ingredients that go into a meal are not the same as the dinner, and the ability to identify the ingredients is not the same as the ability to produce a good meal. One unified creation is preferable to fifty distinct pieces that have little relation to the finished product— or to the process that led to that product.

Many test specialists, confronted by the opposition of writers and writing teachers to their multiple-choice "writing" tests, chalk this view up to prejudice or ignorance. Although prejudice and ignorance may play a role, this opposition mainly reflects a profound difference in assumptions about the nature of writing. Professional writers and writing teachers believe that the writing process is central to writing ability and that the finished product is a complex synthesis, not just the sum of disparate parts. That is why "holistic" reading of essays—the rendering of a single score for the essay as a whole according to fairly general criteria—has become the standard means of scoring essay tests. Whereas multiple-choice tests measure a student's ability to recognize a series of single "right" answers, to demonstrate supposedly discrete skills (such as subject-verb agreement), an essay test measures the student's ability to develop and qualify thought—a quite different activity.

This same difference in assumptions explains why writing teachers are skeptical of multiple-choice measurement concepts when they are used to compare and evaluate different kinds of devices to measure writing ability. For example, using a simple concept of scoring reliability, derived from the notion of single correct answers, some statisticians routinely treat minor differences in judgment of a writing sample as measurement "error."

But such treatment shows that they have misunderstood the kind of reality we are measuring. If we are measuring an objective reality, such as the weight of a piece of metal, a difference in weight on two different scales clearly points to a measurement error (unless we are measuring objects on different planets, which further disturbs the concept of a single objective measurement). The usual item on multiple-choice tests envisions the skill to be measured as the same kind of simple "objective" phenomenon; hence, there is one and only one correct answer hidden among "distractors." But if we are determining the value of a complex phenomenon, such as a writing sample or a work of art, there is probably not a single correct answer or a single right judgment. A difference in judgment is not only *not* error but is positively valuable; the variety of judgments (as experience has shown) helps us see the work in question more clearly and estimate its value more intelligently than a simple unanimity would. (Which is the best Beethoven symphony?) Of course, judgment is not impossible or wholly subjective. (Mozart clearly beats Mancini.) The argument does insist that responsible measurement must be keenly aware of the kind of reality that is being measured. Statistics, with its objective appearance, has a particular responsibility to be theoretically sound in the kinds of evaluation it brings to the testing of writing. (See Shale, 1986, for a model of such responsibility.)

We also need to note the economic and political dimension to these issues. For fifteen years, writing teachers and researchers have been vigorously arguing that they are knowledgeable and sophisticated enough to control testing programs in their field. Even in such large states as New York, New Jersey, and California, writing faculty have become not merely consultants to testing programs but in fact the program directors. The testing professionals, educationists, and statisticians who had become accustomed to directing these programs have watched, in some amazement, as their former authority and former incomes have dwindled. When teachers assert authority over testing programs, it is a kind of class rebellion, more significant in some ways than unionizing for better working conditions. A well-known California university trustee, a wealthy businessman appointed as a reward for his large campaign contributions to a successful governor, nicely summarized the problem when he brushed aside faculty authority over curriculum as "the inmates running the asylum." The surprising success of recent efforts of writing faculty to control testing has in fact made a small but significant dent in the control over education by the usual representatives of the economic and political status quo. In particular, the emphasis on actual writing has on occasion expanded the traditional definition of "good writing" to include some dialectal and scribal patterns that challenge traditional lines of social stratification. (Inner-city or foreign syntax, or a dyslectic spelling problem, may not mean automatic failure, for example.) Thus, writing teachers have actually put into practice some of the concepts of sociolinguistics and social justice that are usually uttered but ignored in our society.

So we should expect that the testing firms and conservative political forces will mount a counterattack. The first signs appeared when educational leaders such as former Education Secretary William Bennett and University of Virginia English Professor E. D. Hirsch called for a return to traditional content, canons, and "cultural literacy." (For a witty response to these arguments, see Robert Pattison's "The Stupidity Crisis," 1988.) The belief, most clearly stated in Hirsch's best-selling book (1987), that one can demonstrate such literacy by identifying terms and by knowing isolated scraps of information returns us to the "trivial pursuits" definition of literacy implied in multiple-choice testing. Another sign, even more ominous, is a book put together by three prominent Educational Testing Service employees, which suggests that mere teachers cannot give responsible writing tests because of certain arcane statistical manipulations that only large testing firms can undertake (Breland and others, 1987). Karen Greenberg, a professor at Hunter College and director of the National Testing Network in Writing, has shown me a draft article in which she argues that the statistics in that book are arranged so as to attack the value of essay testing. If writing teachers are to maintain the influence they now have on the curriculum and testing of writing, they will need to meet this counterattack with vigor, information, and political wisdom.

We do live in a world of practical choices, and there are

no doubt circumstances under which arguments against multiple-choice tests must give way. A responsible multiple-choice test is arguably better than an irresponsible essay test, for most purposes. The multiple-choice tests always produce better-looking numbers, particularly when they measure less meaningful aspects of writing. However, with responsible direct measurement of writing ability now an economical and practical option (see "Organizing and Managing Holistic Essay Readings," White, 1985, pp. 149–169), there is usually no reason to resort to an outdated, reactionary, and often deceptive method of indirect measurement for writing.

The most interesting development in this area is a new attack on essay testing by writing teachers who are uncomfortable with its emphasis on first-draft writing products. (This attack has been invited, in part, by an overenthusiastic defense of essay testing on the part of its proponents, including me.) New kinds of measures, such as portfolio or process folder evaluations, are being proposed, in an attempt to reflect more accurately the thinking and revising process that is essential to the development of writing ability (Faigley and others, 1985). Adopting a concept familiar in the fine arts, evaluators of portfolios assess several examples of student work, including multiple versions of the same piece. The two most prominent experiments using such devices are the upper-division writing certification program at the State University of New York at Stony Brook and the entry-level placement program at the University of Minnesota. As with essay testing twenty-five years ago, these experimental measurement devices will need to demonstrate reasonable economy and reliability before they are likely to be widely used.

Norm Referencing Versus Criterion Referencing

Norm-referenced testing, the standard method of mental measurement since the model was developed for aptitude testing of World War I draftees, has a superficial appeal for the testing of writing. It suggests such virtues as objectivity, comparability, and statistical complexity. However, such testing has some serious problems, particularly for those seeking to measure student writing ability for instructional purposes.

Most multiple-choice tests (but not all) are norm referenced; that is, they assume a "normal" distribution of the skills measured, which means in practical terms that they are designed to produce a bell curve. Thus, if you score at the tenth percentile on a test of mechanical ability, 90 percent of the population has greater mechanical aptitude than you, and you should be kept away from valuable equipment. In order to produce a bell curve, the test design requires a preponderance of questions that about half of the test population will answer correctly, with a few very easy questions (to produce the left-hand slope of the curve) and a few very hard questions (for the right-hand slope). If the curve becomes distorted, as it may if too many students answer too many questions correctly or incorrectly, the test is revised to reestablish the normal curve. Furthermore, the curve (against which all other test takers will be compared) is determined by the ability and (sometimes even more significantly) the aptitude and upbringing of the norming population.

Since norm referencing assumes a "normal" distribution of the skills it measures, it is disrupted by education; even short-term training can alter some score distributions and skew the bell curve. So such tests attempt to discount the effects of education in order to preserve the purity of the model. That situation is particularly unfortunate for the testing of writing, since writing "aptitude" as defined by these tests will often reflect the economic, social, or ethnic conditions of the home at the time the student was learning the language; whatever discounts school learning in the measurement of writing ability tends to benefit the already advantaged.

Although I am not suggesting that norm referencing is either evil or necessarily inappropriate in all cases, I am pointing out the potential problems for those who would measure writing ability by a norm-referenced test. The norming population must be a primary concern. For example, when a test normed on eastern prep school students is used on a less advantaged group of students, the results probably will be distorted if the test contains the usual number of questions calling for cultural advantages and an ear for the privileged dialect. For various reasons, students from minority cultures seem to score particularly poorly on such tests, despite relatively normal distributions on writing sample tests (White, 1985, pp. 71–83; Koenig and Mitchell, 1988).

Even if the norming group seems an appropriate one, the test still may include items that reflect aptitude or social class rather than writing ability. Here, for example, is a sample question adapted from a popular test designed to measure college-level competence in English composition:

> English-speaking musicians use in their profession large numbers of words from which one of the following languages?
> a. German
> b. French
> c. Spanish
> d. Latin
> e. Italian

The test makers are obviously looking in this question for a scrap of information about the ways in which English uses foreign words—in this case the Italian vocabulary for some aspects of musical notation. Some students might pick up such information in a composition course, though it seems unlikely; but the student most able to darken the proper space on an answer sheet is probably the one whose parents wanted to and could afford to give him or her classical music lessons as a child. Those who were not so privileged (including, no doubt, some performing musicians) are not likely to know the answer, regardless of their writing ability. And someone who knows too much—say a specialist in medieval music—might even give the "wrong" answer, Latin.

It would be easy to select other bad items from norm-referenced tests, particularly items that are culture linked, such as the one above, or items based on dialect or usage differences that have no bearing on writing ability. Norm referencing encourages such items because they "work" for certain convenient norming populations. (Essay testing has its share, and more, of bad questions, but they tend to be so difficult to score consistently that they are rarely repeated; essay readers are much more opinionated and vocal than are the computers that score multiple-choice answer sheets.)

Those who are not specialists in testing sometimes fail to realize how narrowly and precisely conceived the most professional norm-referenced tests are. I once asked an ETS test specialist about a particular item on the Scholastic Aptitude Test. "It's really a stupid question," I said to him, in some exasperation. He cheerfully agreed. "Sure is. But those who succeed in the first year of college get it right, and those who don't succeed get it wrong. And that's what the test is all about." He was right, in a narrow sense, since ETS consistently tries to make those who use, and misuse, the SAT understand that its sole purpose is to predict success in the first year of college. But no amount of information seems to keep people from imagining that the SAT is a general intelligence test or (even worse) a proficiency test for the nation's high schools.

Those who select norm-referenced tests to measure their students' writing abilities usually recognize the problems inherent in the construction and the norming populations of these tests. However, they argue, the tests are readily available, inexpensive, and convenient. These are not trivial arguments. It is up to those informed about writing to make a case for high-quality assessments in their field. Just as other parts of the institution will argue for high-quality paint or equipment, on the grounds that shoddy materials cost more in the long run, so writing teachers and informed administrators need to document the costs to education of inappropriate norm-referenced tests, however cheap and handy they may be.

If, as is usually the case, existing norm-referenced tests do not meet local test specifications or are not appropriate for the particular test population, it is time to consider adopting criterion-referenced testing—that is, testing according to standards defined without reference to a student population. Criterion-referenced tests do not seek to obtain a normal curve, since they are directed to the material of a course of instruction or a body of knowledge. Those who have not learned the material will turn out very poor responses, while those who have mastered the material will do extremely well. A skewed curve, therefore, does not mean a badly constructed test but, rather, a test group that either knows the material or does not.

The particular advantage of criterion-referenced testing is obvious: the questions can be developed directly out of stated test criteria and for the specific purposes of the particular test or testing program. The disadvantage of such testing is equally obvious: since it is highly unlikely that a criterion-referenced test for a specific purpose will be available commercially, tests usually must be developed, and the statistical comfort of national normative data will not be available. In test construction, the danger comes from the use of unrealistic or unfair criteria, or from criteria that may be fair for one population but not another.

Since essay tests combine the advantages of norm referencing and criterion referencing, usually emphasizing the criteria, many institutions and many state programs have adopted such tests in recent years. Almost without exception, they have found that essay tests yield useful and credible scores as well as major benefits in faculty development and curricular change. Where such testing has generated faculty resistance, the objections have centered on the perceived rigidity of the criteria, which, without the moderating influence of norm referencing, may work to the disadvantage of some elements of the population.

The debate between criterion referencing and norm referencing of writing tests often develops into an argument between the advocates of essay and multiple-choice testing; but the two issues are not altogether the same. It is perfectly possible to develop criterion-referenced multiple-choice tests, and it is (unfortunately) becoming more and more common to adopt an essay test with its norms and statistics from some other program. Both criterion and norm referencing have their value, of course, as well as their problems; difficulties arise for those who fail to be clear conceptually about which kind of test they are giving, or the degree to which they are combining both kinds.

In holistic essay testing, which blends criterion and norm referencing, the scoring guide sets out the criteria for scoring, while the ranking of papers against each other in accordance with sample papers tends toward the normative. Since a decision about the meaning of the holistic ranking takes place after the scoring is completed, those in charge can moderate the impersonality of the criteria by the humanity of the actual performance, or they can adjust the statistics of the score distribution according to the professionalism of the criteria. The flexibility of holistic essay testing allows those evaluating student writing to design the kind of test that will meet the needs of their particular students and program.

Correctness Versus Discovery, Thought, and Organization

In Chapter Four, we looked at some of the reasons for the persistence of workbook grammar and usage instruction in the teaching of writing, despite the well-demonstrated ineffectiveness of those curricula. Many of the same arguments apply in the assessment of writing, though they do not work in quite the same way. A test that requires a student to identify errors in a prose passage or a group of sentences is not measuring that student's ability to create or develop ideas, or even to produce error-free prose. Every writing teacher knows students who can identify the usual errors on tests but who commit the same errors regularly while writing. Nonetheless, the evaluation of writing is irrevocably linked to the concept of error, no matter how hard we may try to separate editing from writing first drafts.

Every sensible person knows that readers will react negatively to a piece of writing that contains numerous mechanical errors. One constant in student mythology about writing is "Neatness counts." Evidence from essay readings suggests that there is an element of truth in this mythology. Even first-draft test writing requires a certain standard of spelling, punctuation, sentence structure, and clear vocabulary if it is to be evaluated favorably by readers looking for developed thought. Thus, the apparent polarization between those concerned about measuring usage or correctness and those interested in more substantive matters tends to disappear in the actual grading of student essays.

In the California study of writing programs (White and Polin, 1986), sophisticated and trained readers graded over three thousand essays according to three scoring guides. The researchers were surprised to find that the scores on the holistic scale (which urged readers to subordinate mechanical matters to more substantial issues) correlated somewhat more strongly with a scale called "Correctness and Efficiency" (.56) than with one called "Development and Focus" (.47). That is, despite the instructions on the scoring guide, trained readers giving holistic scores on the overall quality of a piece of first-draft test prose paid a bit more attention to mechanics and accuracy than they did to structural matters.

The underlying issue here concerns the place of usage and correctness in the teaching of writing in college. That is, where and how should correctness and usage be taught? Research shows that direct instruction in these matters simply does not affect writing, and most faculties believe that these matters belong properly to the schools, not the colleges. Traditionally, then, these matters are remanded to "remedial" programs, often without baccalaureate credit, taught by the least well-trained and poorest-paid teachers. These programs, again traditionally, repeat the workbook grammar that has spectacularly failed the remedial students in the past.

The California study suggests that most such "remedial" programs are ineffective because they assume that correctness must be taught before more substantive matters can be dealt with. Just as the researchers were surprised at the relatively high correlation of the Correctness and Efficiency scale with the holistic one, they were also surprised that the mean score on the Correctness and Efficiency scale was lower than that on the Development and Focus scale (7.68 on a twelve-point scale, as opposed to 7.95). After analysis of the relationship between these two scales, the researchers concluded that the difference in performance on the two scales was particularly significant for the weakest writers—those with low scores on Correctness and Efficiency despite their remedial training. For these students, the report recommends a different approach to remediation, delaying intensive work on sentence and word problems and focusing first on invention and structure of ideas. Traditional remediation, with its unremitting emphasis on correctness, "seems to be not only ineffective but also deadening to the mind and spirit." But if the program delays the direct teaching of correctness, it can find much to build upon. "Some of the weakest writers in our sample, those with low scores on [Correctness and Efficiency] despite their remedial training, showed a surprising ability to use rhetorical markers, shift levels of abstraction, and focus their arguments" (White and Polin, 1986, vol. 1, pp. 316–317).

The findings of this study (and many others—for instance, Krashen, Scarcella, and Long, 1982) suggest that the acquisition (that is, absorption rather than direct learning) of correctness is a *result* of reading and writing rather than a prerequisite for reading and writing. The curricular implication is that college remedial programs should focus on appropriate reading and writing, not on workbook drill. If we accept into our institutions students who regularly commit the familiar correctness errors, we must understand that only years of steady experience with college-level reading, writing, and revision will reduce the level of error to manageable and acceptable proportions. If correctness in written work is required for success in the undergraduate curriculum (as it normally is), the remedial curriculum needs to be intellectually challenging, so that students will be able to spend several terms in it, if necessary, acquiring the needed mechanical skill without becoming stigmatized or brain dead from boredom. In most cases, in short, the remedial curriculum can be college level and stimulating, for teachers as well as students, even as it indirectly insists on a necessary correctness in its students' writing products.

The assessment implication is also clear: placement tests ought not to focus on error, as they now do, but should use larger concepts of writing as a thinking process. The particular value of the Development and Focus scale (White and Polin, 1986, vol. 1, pp. 135–142; an early version appears in White, 1985, pp. 145–147) for placement purposes is that it seeks to distinguish among the students according to the complexity of their ability to think systematically. Such a placement device allows groupings that make sense for a curriculum based on reading and writing; it also subordinates, without wholly ignoring, correctness issues. Colleges, however, need not adopt this particular scale; any challenging writing task, scored with attention to the student's thinking process, will allow for a similar placement procedure. Above all, we should stop classifying all students with spelling or mechanical difficulties as "boneheads," and we should stop using assessment devices that focus wholly or principally on correctness.

Teacher Involvement in Testing Programs

Since most teachers of writing have little training, and little interest, in testing, administrators are tempted to place testing programs entirely in the hands of professional test makers or campus test specialists. To be sure, many of those who teach writing consider the measurement of writing ability irrelevant to their task or even inimical to it. If they are to help students write more effectively, they believe, they should stay away from evaluation, which many students associate with negative responses or even with failure. I have considerable sympathy for this view, supported as it is by much inappropriate testing and insensitive use of grades; but I want to argue here that good measurement practice involves much more than sorting and grading and can help writing teachers in important ways. That is, when teachers are involved in the testing of writing, the tests are likely to be much improved and the teaching surely will be improved by what participating teachers learn. Teachers who have worked on holistic essay tests bring back to their classrooms ideas from these tests that improve their teaching substantially.

In the first place, experience with a testing program helps writing teachers attend to the writing and revision of writing assignments, a problem I discussed at length in the previous chapter. When these teachers begin to adapt the more rigorous standards of a testing program to their classroom assignments, they find that the usual unclear writing topic—presented to students orally rather than in written form—will no longer do. Quite naturally, these teachers begin to revise the assignments they give their students and hence improve their teaching. But this is only the first of the changes that can emerge when teachers become involved in testing.

One of the most interesting grade appeal cases I have been involved with occurred when I was chairman of an English department. A student who received an *F* on a perfectly appalling term paper claimed that it was really worth an *A*. As evidence, she brought two different statements of praise accompanied by the grade of *A* that the paper had previously received from two other teachers in other courses, one taken at another university. While there was a certain grim comedy involved in this case of the much-used all-purpose term paper, it was, of course, just a local example of what Paul Diederich (1974) demonstrated to be generally true when he began research into essay scoring: without clear grading criteria, all papers will receive all possible scores. Our students in general believe, on the basis of their experience, that grades for writing are unpredictable, arbitrary, inconsistent, and normally a matter of luck more than skill. Most observers of teacher grading agree that in this respect the students are absolutely right. Therefore, since students do not—and often cannot—know what we want, they tend to confuse plagiarism with research, passivity with seriousness, neatness with quality of prose, and fulfillment of the word count with fulfillment of the assignment. The thriving market in commercially or fraternally produced term papers is mute testimony to the interchangeability of our assignments and the lack of clarity of our grading standards. Nancy Sommers (1982, p. 153) notes, in another context, that vagueness is routinely forbidden to student writers but remains the property of their teachers.

Some surveys have shown that almost all the time spent by teachers in what they call "teaching writing" is in fact spent grading papers. Much of that time is wasted, wasted by inscribing endless red marks that the students almost always entirely ignore or misunderstand. The grades on these red-marked papers seem to the students to emerge out of private and unknowable quirkiness, from an unaccountable censoriousness that they remember when they later see us at social occasions. ("You're an English teacher? I'd better watch what I say!") Meanwhile, their overworked teachers tell us they are too busy teaching writing to get involved with measurement; too busy at busywork undertaken for their own amusement (for why else do these martyrs spend every weekend grading papers, "bleeding all over them," as some put it, working endless hours); too busy to realize that they need to know about such measurement devices as scoring guides in order to work effectively and efficiently. Writing teachers who participate in holistic essay-scoring sessions are prepared to change these self-defeating behaviors.

A teacher involved in the construction of essay tests will soon realize that scoring reliability is both necessary for the sake of fairness and achievable with some effort—achievable if one produces a well-developed assignment with clear demands and goals and a clearly articulated set of scoring criteria, usually embodied in a written scoring guide that can be illustrated by sample student essays at each score point. We know now that readers who follow such a set of scoring criteria, under conditions controlling other outside variables, can achieve extremely consistent grading (White, 1985, pp. 177–180).

Teachers who have participated in developing or scoring essay tests inevitably begin to use what they have learned in their own teaching. A teacher will often pass through three stages in the process. During the first stage, the teacher becomes acutely aware of the need for consistent grading and draws up a set of criteria (or a scoring guide) for use while reading and grading student papers. Since fairness is not a trivial matter, some teachers also try to eliminate the variables that may keep them from grading student work according to the standards on their scoring guide. For example, some teachers will find ways to conceal the student's name on submitted work, since they suspect that previous grades will influence the scoring of the present paper. (I must say that I do not go to this extreme, since I see my comments on student papers as a kind of continuing dialogue with my students; I try to find ways to compliment them on improvement.)

But this concentration on a developed scoring guide for the assignment leads quickly to a second stage. Once the scoring criteria have become clear enough to the teacher to be set down in writing, why not share them with the students? In fact, why not share them with the students early in the writing process, so that they can know from the outset the standards for judgment to which they will be subject? Indeed, why not involve the students themselves in the *creation* of the scoring guide, so that they can see the quality standards as partly of their own devising? Teachers who use scoring guides in this way spend more time working with students as they write their papers, since the standards for performance are clear and public, and the students are more ready to seek help in meeting them.

A third stage then beckons. Since the standards of judgment are both clear and public, and since they have at least in part been developed by the class, we can now ask the class members to respond to and score the essays written by their peers. Since the students now have both a vocabulary and a scale to use in discussing and evaluating the writing they examine, they no longer deliver only the positive and unhelpful comments that Hillocks derides (see Chapter Three). Instead, they can (and in fact do) hold the other students' essays to the standards set out in the guide. Moreover, by learning how to read and evaluate the papers written by other students, they learn how to read their own. This procedure has the magical double value of increasing student learning at the same time that it decreases the teacher's paper load. Although few teachers will want to use peer grading for final drafts or for crucial course grade decisions, many teachers find that students write better drafts for peer groups than for the instructor and that they gain more from a peer group's critique than from the instructor's written comments.

Students' revisions (discussed in Chapter Four) also seem to improve as a result of the new insights that writing teachers gain from participation in testing. Normally, even good students will not revise their work because they don't see anything wrong with it. They look at their work, however filled with original sins, and, like another Creator, pronounce it very good.

They may, if they are diligent students, be willing to change things around to please the teacher in order to get a better grade; but they do not believe that revision will really help them write better. One way to get students to revise their work adequately is to teach them enough about evaluation of writing so that they can see what needs improvement in their own drafts. The half-hearted tinkering that most good students do to please us— often worsening rather than improving their work—has little to do with real revision, which must respond to internal needs, a felt sense that improvement is both possible and noticeable. Teachers who are hostile to or uninformed about evaluation— that is, most writing teachers—are ill equipped to help students in this way. Students cannot learn about the evaluation of writing—why some essays deserve high grades and others deserve low grades—unless the teachers know why themselves and can make that knowledge clear, consistent, and public.

Teacher involvement with testing programs can thus do much more than bring practical knowledge to the assessment. The training that the teachers acquire as they work to develop and score a careful test supports the best goals of the teaching of writing: thoughtful and precise assignments, fair and public grading criteria, and a curriculum that leads to self-assessment and natural revision of work by the students. Responsible bookkeeping would reduce the cost of a writing test program by the value of such a faculty development program.

High Cost and High Validity Versus Cheap Testing

The arguments against conventional norm-referenced, multiple-choice tests of usage and mechanics are so strong that virtually the only arguments for them are convenience and cost. They are so cheap and handy, particularly the worst of them, that they have all the appeal of a McDonald's hamburger. Although convenience and cost are not to be sneered at, no sensible person makes them the only criteria for action. But when decision makers are not informed about the problems such tests (or such hamburgers) create, their appeal is almost irresistible. In fact, however, most institutions have moved beyond this

level into different varieties of direct measurement, all of which
also have cost implications.

If the decision is to proceed with an essay test, administrators need to recognize that a substantial investment of faculty time will be required. The responsible committee will need
to develop substantial expertness in the testing of writing and
undertake each of the following steps in sequence:

1. Committee meetings and institutional decisions about the
    goals and criteria for the test.
2. Committee meetings and decisions acting on the prior deci-
    sions about goals and criteria: What kinds of questions are
    to be asked? How many separate essays are to be required?
    How long is the test to be? How will it be administered?
    When is it to be given and scored?
3. Implementation of the new decisions by specific specialist
    bodies: test development committees; test-scoring leaders;
    support teams for printing, proctoring, and the like.
4. Preparation of materials for prospective test takers, includ-
    ing sample questions and scoring criteria; preparation of a
    score-reporting system that takes into account both institu-
    tional and instructional purposes.

Since my previous book goes into considerable detail on
these matters (White, 1985), I will not repeat that discussion
here. But the last point requires some amplification, since the
distinction between institutional and instructional purposes for
testing is often not clearly understood.

When institutions develop tests, they are primarily concerned with institutional needs. That is, they want to group students of like abilities for efficiency of instruction; or they want
to withhold the baccalaureate degree from students who cannot
write, since such students will embarrass the institution. These
and other institutional goals are reasonable and appropriate, and
do in fact work for the benefit of most students as well. But no
one should think that institutional needs are the same as individual needs. Thus, although it is surely to the benefit of the institution to ensure that degree recipients can read and write well,

such a goal directly frustrates the weak student's drive to the degree. Humane and responsible administrators will be keenly aware of that drive, and of the conflict with the institution that the student faces, and will support the testing program with counseling appointments, individual study opportunities, alternative ways of proving writing ability, appeals procedures, upper-division writing courses, and the like. If the testing program is designed for instructional as well as institutional goals, it will motivate the student to improve and will also provide instructional options so that the desire to improve can be fulfilled.

We cannot discuss testing costs without considering the individual as well as the institutional implications, the effects on teachers and students as well as the statistical reports. If we were to think only of giving a test and reporting scores, cost comparisons would be easy. But a serious testing program involves much more than handing out the pencils and mailing the computer printouts. The committee seeking approval of a goals statement is really reviewing the purposes of the institution; the test development committee is incidentally revising course curricula and undergoing faculty development; the team working on options for those who fail the test is developing social policy and priorities for the college; those scoring an essay test are learning new skills for the teaching of writing. How can we compare costs for such activities to the cost of running answer sheets through a machine? How can we tally the benefits of expenditures on such a program separately from all the other activities of the institution?

Thus, the issue of cost for a writing test program cannot be separated from institutional goals and priorities. If there is agreement that writing is a crucial part of learning, that the development of thought is more important than the accumulation of information, that students are expected to be active participants in their own learning, then a program that uses direct measurement is an incredible bargain. When the costs of the program are seen as too high, writing itself—and not merely the test—is being defined as expendable.

A striking example of setting priorities creatively in this area is occurring as this book goes to press. As mentioned earlier in this chapter, the University of Minnesota has announced that it will use *portfolio evaluation* as the placement test for its incoming freshmen. The procedure is, as so far developed, extremely expensive and unreliable; however, it has one overriding benefit that, this university believes, overwhelms all else: Students who are required to present portfolios of their writing on admission to college will understand that writing is essential to their education. Those who are developing the procedures admit that cheating is bound to occur, that the expense of reading some thousands of portfolios is very high, that criteria for evaluation are uncertain at best. But the effects of that placement procedure (now widely publicized in the area) are already clear. The high schools are now forced to emphasize writing, so that students can put together the necessary portfolios. Neither multiple-choice tests (which do not encourage writing) nor tests of first-draft writing (which are more effective but still not powerful enough) have led to the kind of preparation for college that this institution wants to see. This university has decided to put the instructional purpose of the placement procedure ahead of the institutional purpose—so far ahead that the endurance of the experiment (funded in part from an outside grant) must remain in doubt.

Test professionals throw up their hands in despair at programs so "unprofessional." From their perspective, there can be no assurance that students are being treated fairly (how can reliability data be collected?), and even the proposed gains in student writing cannot be accurately measured when the portfolios vary widely in size, mode, and authenticity. These are not trivial complaints. They stem from the behavioral and empirical assumptions about human behavior and institutions—statistical and social-scientific assumptions that have led to vast progress of a certain sort. But serious educators must reiterate and demonstrate that these assumptions are not the only possible ones and that the progress they have brought us has been purchased at great cost. "That which is measurable," goes the old saying, "drives out that which is important." It sometimes seems as if the institutions that we thought were there to help us do our work have become our masters; the institution has its own agenda, priorities, and goals, and they are not always the same as ours or our students'.

However, educational and institutional needs frequently intersect. We weaken our institutions at our peril, and if we argue too strenuously against their interests, we become irrelevant. As we do our best to select, score, and use the results of assessment devices within our institutions, we need to keep the interests of the students prominently before us. We cannot simply yield these professional concerns and human values to testing services and institutional managers.

Chapter 6

Using Tests
for Admissions, Placement,
and Instructional Evaluation

The testing of student writing ability serves many different functions for colleges and universities. While few institutions will assess student writing ability for all of the following purposes, most will use assessment for several of them: (1) admissions, (2) placement, (3) freshman composition equivalency, (4) exit from remedial or freshman composition courses, (5) certification of "rising junior" and upper-division writing proficiency, and (6) demonstration of "value added" for individuals or for programs (as in program evaluation). Writing tests sometimes are selected by institutions, or are imposed on institutions, without much regard for these differing purposes; as a result, the testing may be inappropriate and invalid and may not support the teaching of writing. Each purpose calls for different kinds of testing, validation, and institutional arrangement.

For each of these kinds of tests, we can find two general and (sometimes) conflicting goals: (1) the administrative goal of selecting and classifying people and (2) the instructional goal of helping students learn more effectively (see Brown, 1986). The two goals may coincide; for instance, an effective placement test allows the institution to proceed more efficiently with relatively homogeneous groupings of students, and it enables students to learn more efficiently in classes suited to their preparation. But frequently the administrative goal supersedes or

113

conflicts with instructional goals; that is, admissions tests may be designed to keep students out, and exit proficiency tests may be designed to withhold certification from the undeserving. Clearly, the best testing programs will seek to bring the administrative and instructional goals as close together as possible.

Admissions

The two national admissions testing programs both test verbal ability through multiple-choice formats. Half of the College Board's Scholastic Aptitude Test (SAT) measures verbal aptitude, and the American College Testing Program (ACT) offers similar assessment. In both cases, the tests do not, and do not pretend to, measure writing ability. While there is some unstated and unclear relationship between these measures and the ability to write, both testing agencies are careful to state that the tests are general aptitude tests designed to predict success in college—that is, the student's ability to make it through the first year.

Many misconceptions about these aptitude tests and their relationship to writing are current, most particularly from those who imagine that the tests examine more than they do. No one is quite sure just what it is that allows students to succeed in college, but almost everyone is aware that no single test can measure whatever it is. Certainly, verbal and mathematical aptitudes play a role, as do finances, motivation, parental involvement, and social maturity. The simple ability to pass multiple-choice tests is clearly important. These tests attempt, with some success, to correlate with student persistence and hence to approach this complex construct that leads to college success. But that is all they do, and—as recent protests about their underprediction for women have demonstrated—even this limited goal is imperfectly realized. It is as invalid to read these admissions tests as tests of writing ability (and thus to use them for placement or equivalency for freshman English) as it is to call them scorecards for the nation's high schools (as some politicians do).

The use of these tests as if they were writing tests suggests (whatever cautions may be articulated) that college writing has something important to do with guessing correct answers; such a message is surely a destructive one. The even less defensible use of these tests as pretest/posttest measures assumes that somehow writing instruction will improve aptitude for college study, and that we can evaluate the writing program by measuring changes in aptitude, despite the fact that these aptitude tests are specifically designed *not* to show the effects of learning. It is usually a very bad idea to use a test designed for one purpose for some other purpose.

Thus, I will not discuss here the many complicated issues about the use of multiple-choice admissions tests. Both critics and defenders agree that the scores are, in one way or another, less reliable for cultural and racial minorities and that they should never be used alone to make admissions decisions. The College Board, despite its public stance that the SAT should not be seen as diagnostic, has blurred the distinction between the exclusionary function of the admissions test and a placement function; overzealous representatives of the Board have argued for the use of the SAT instead of valid placement tests, and the Board has attached a linguistically suspect "Test of Standard Written English" to the SAT. My concern here has only to do with the use of these admissions tests as if they were writing tests, which they are not.

Aside from this dubious use of verbal aptitude measures, writing assessment for admission takes two forms: (1) personal statements written (supposedly) by applicants to accompany applications for admission and (2) formal testing of writing by the law and medical schools.

The personal statements sent along with applications for admission to colleges and professional schools are often, committee members will say, very revealing. Unfortunately, there is no consistent way to know quite what they reveal. The directions for such statements are often vague, so that the responses will differ in kind as well as in quality. Canny applicants will routinely solicit help, which ranges from editing to ghost writing, in producing the statements, so that their authenticity is always in doubt. And, finally, the criteria for evaluating the statements are normally so highly subjective (and unstated) that reliable judgment is not to be expected; amateur psychologizing occasionally rears its Freudian head, and such qualities as "sincerity" or "proper" moral stances sometimes influence naive judgments of the work.

Dissatisfied in part with the use of personal statements, and uncertain about their meaning, the Association of American Medical Colleges instituted large-scale research into an essay portion for the Medical College Admissions Test (MCAT) in 1985. (The medical schools also hoped that the essay portion of the MCAT would suggest the importance of a broad education to premedical students.) As this book goes to press, it is unclear whether that experiment will lead to a permanent written essay on the MCAT, though some form of direct measurement of writing seems a probable outcome. But numbers of medical college admissions committees have responded favorably to the dependable and new information that a structured, timed, secure, and defined writing test gives them. The Law School Admissions Test (LSAT) also includes an essay portion.

The essay tests have added consistency and security to the written portion of the MCAT and the LSAT, but the test developers have not yet decided on reliable ways to use these essays. The law school test is, at this writing, simply sent to admissions committees, to be used as they wish. The medical schools have developed large scored samples for research purposes after each administration of the test during the study period. Some admissions committees found that the essay tests maintain most of the advantages of the personal statement and add to them the controls of a testing situation; however, outside the controlled scoring session, inconsistent and idiosyncratic evaluation of the essays poses a major problem. The solution to this problem is clear: reliable centralized scoring sessions under professional direction, as the study sample has demonstrated (Mitchell and Anderson, 1986; Koenig and Mitchell, 1988). The MCAT studies have shown that reliable and economical scoring of large numbers of admissions essay tests for professional schools is feasible. Since the validity of a measure can be no greater than the reliability of its scoring, it seems logical that the next step in the use of essays for admissions purposes will be the institution of a carefully designed and scored writing sample as supplement to the elusive personal statement.

Placement

Most colleges and universities now place students into appropriate writing courses by means of a writing test. The practice is by now so well accepted, and its hundred-year history so established (Gere, 1985a), that few question either why or how it is done. Such inattention to placement can lead to major problems. One large state university, for example, "places" students in remedial classes by means of a state department of education test that no one on campus (as far as I could tell on a campus evaluation visit) had ever seen; though everyone agreed that a substantial group of students needed remediation, this placement was only advisory, since neither the placement test nor the rudimentary remedial program had received much attention. The quite remarkable disarray of the entire composition program could in part be traced to this neglect of the placement issue, which everyone on campus thought someone else was attending to. The teaching assistants assigned to the freshman composition course told us (in private) that the course was very difficult to teach, since the wide range of ability levels forced them to ignore some of the students. Under such circumstances, the weakest students tend to receive the most attention, since they are at risk of failure, while the strong students receive little challenge. We heard constant complaints from the faculty in general about the low level of competence shown even by students who passed freshman composition with good grades. A careful placement test and a remedial program connected to the test would be a wise and economical investment for this campus.

We will look again at the placement issue in the following chapter, which focuses on the organization of writing programs. But here, in the testing context, it is important to remind ourselves that placement makes sense only if there are both an identifiable group of students who require special support and a professional support program in place. Before either of these matters can be attended to, the required freshman composition program ought to be defined with a kind of precision rare in American education. As frequently happens, attention to testing leads directly to definition and often revision of the entire writing curriculum.

Administrators or faculty outside of English are likely to believe that someone can come up with an objective definition of "remedial writing." It relates, they imagine, to the material taught in high school, which, of course, ought not to be college-level study. Thus, some mathematics faculty will argue, all math below calculus must be considered remedial. But American education is not structured that way, most particularly in its two foundation disciplines, English and mathematics. In both of these fields, the work done by, and expected of, the best high school seniors is at a higher level than what we find in most first-year college courses. Only selective institutions can maintain the belief that all students unready for calculus are "remedial"; when we seek the parallel to that standard for writing, we wind up in some educational, social, and economic difficulties.

The fact is that there is no single, context-free definition of "remedial writing." Since every institution, or system, needs to develop an operational definition of the term, the obvious place to start is with the regular freshman composition program. A remedial student is one who lacks whatever it is that is expected of those *entering* the regular program—not, we need to remind ourselves, of those *completing* the program. The answers to this question are easily obtained if one asks the right people: those who are teaching the students in question.

For example, after a series of meetings, the composition faculty from one moderately selective university gave a fairly simple response to the central question. I kept asking them during the meetings, "What distinguishes students who are ready to do the work in your regular course from those who are not?" The answer emerged after a serious curriculum review: basic sentence-level skills. I was surprised; this was not an open-enrollment institution. Nonetheless, instruction in the regular composition course began with paragraph construction and focused on ways of demonstrating ideas in the paragraph and (later) in the essay. Besides, I was informed, a great many of the freshmen who met university entrance requirements had serious problems at the word and sentence level, so that there seemed no point in examining for more advanced skills.

The natural next step was to devise a placement examination that examined these word- and sentence-level skills. Within a year, such a test was created, pretested, and administered. True enough, close to half of the entering students scored at the remedial level. But the story does not end there. The remedial course now had some clear goals, and the institution put some real resources behind the effort to reach those goals: class size was limited to twelve, renewed attention was given to the tutorial/ learning center, experimentation was encouraged, and regular faculty were rewarded for participating. The remedial course, under these encouraging conditions, was now able to bring most of its students not only up to the expected level but well beyond. Before five years had passed, those teaching the regular freshman course had reexamined and upgraded its curriculum, and the schools preparing students for the university were enhancing their writing programs in order to ensure that their students would pass the test. At this writing, the test is under review to see whether it should include more advanced skills, and a new study skills course has been established for students who are not ready to begin work at the "remedial" level.

The most important issue in placement testing stands out clearly from these contrasting experiences. Institutions that seek to save money by adopting outside placement tests without much attention normally gain only administrative sorting from such tests—and sometimes not even that. But institutions that are willing to see the placement test as functionally related to the writing program wind up not only with more appropriate tests but also with a natural and continuing program review.

Moreover, placement tests deliver a powerful message to the schools. If there is no writing on the placement test, the schools preparing students for college have little incentive to require the steady writing that leads to real improvement. This message function of placement has led some institutions to experiment with the portfolio assessment I described in Chapter Five; certainly, many years of multiple-choice testing have diminished the importance of writing for college preparation, and the reverse may indeed occur.

Those evaluating the effectiveness of placement testing in writing need to be particularly aware of the difference between placement and admissions testing. Predictive validity is essential for admissions tests; their function is to separate potential winners from losers, and the results at the end of the freshman year should correlate highly with test scores. But placement tests exist to turn potential losers into winners. An effective remedial program will defeat the predictions of placement testing; that is, it will help students succeed when (according to the predictions of placement) they were supposed to fail. A naive evaluation of the placement program based on simple predictive validity not only ignores the effects of remedial instruction but declares that the program has the best statistics when it works the least well.

Equivalency

Equivalency testing is similar to but essentially different from placement testing. Whereas placement testing seeks to discover readiness for entrance into a curriculum, equivalency testing discovers whether the student already knows what that curriculum is designed to teach. Thus, equivalency testing provides both university credit by examination and placement of the student into the next course. In addition, placement testing is directly related to student learning, which it is designed to support, whereas equivalency testing is almost purely administrative, saying "yes" or "no" to students who believe they can "challenge" coursework they have not taken but whose goals they have met outside the classroom.

There are two ways in which students gain equivalency credit: (1) through outside examinations based on a generalized curriculum and (2) through challenge tests administered by the institution and based on the particular goals of a campus course. Each of these methods has its own advantages and disadvantages.

The two national equivalency testing programs are administered by the Educational Testing Service (ETS) for the College Board: the Advanced Placement Program (AP) and the College-

Level Examination Program (CLEP). A third large-scale program that is designed to offer credit for freshman composition has been developed by the English faculty of the California State University, the English Equivalency Examination (EEE), which is offered once a year in California only. All three of these programs offer examinations intended to discover whether a student has achieved the general goals of freshman composition. Each recommends that those passing receive six semester units of credit by examination.

The AP exam is the oldest of these tests. For three decades, it has been fostering AP courses in high schools, based on a traditional college freshman English course. Recently, the program has offered two options, one in literature and the other in composition. Students completing the AP course then take one of the two exams, which include both multiple-choice and essay portions. The scores are converted to a five-point scale, with 5 as the best; normally, universities will grant credit for scores of 3, 4, or 5. From time to time, some universities register unease with AP standards, but in general the program has worked very well: the courses tend to be oases of quality in a barren senior year of high school (for both students and teachers), and those passing the difficult tests have shown that they are indeed ready for more advanced work. The problem with AP is that it is based in high school courses and hence reflects the economic and racial biases of the society: the more privileged students tend to attend the high schools able to afford this enriched curriculum.

CLEP originated as part of the credit-by-examination program offered to members of the military and was later adopted by ETS as an attempt to offer college credit outside the structure of the AP course. (It is possible in theory to take an AP exam without taking an AP course, but hardly anyone does.) The College Board still later decided to sponsor CLEP as well as AP, though the Board has never been particularly comfortable with CLEP's relatively unstructured base and less elitist approach to college work. Indeed, those who think that the College Board and ETS are the same are unaware of the conflicts between New York and Princeton on equivalency testing; even on ETS's comfortable Princeton campus, the bureaucratic infighting between AP and CLEP, particularly in the 1970s, has been fierce. In recent years, College Board committees have sought to align the AP and CLEP tests in such areas as English; but the two programs remain alive, competing with each other and serving different needs. CLEP offers a General Examination in English Composition and several Subject Examinations (longer, and more difficult) in the field. Responding to pressure from faculty, CLEP added a centrally scored written portion to its multiple-choice General Examination for one administration a year. The Subject Examinations provide for a written portion, but the receiving institution must score it. The American Council on Education has recommended credit-level scores for each of the examinations, and institutions can safely allow credit for these careful tests, as long as the written portions are scored and meet the college's standards.

The EEE was developed as a reaction to widespread use of an early form of the CLEP General Examination in English Composition, a short multiple-choice usage test. The California English faculty—arguing that any test offering credit for college English must test actual writing and reading—developed a test made up of two forty-five-minute essay questions and a ninety-minute test of reading (the CLEP Subject Examination on "Analysis and Interpretation of Literature"). As with the AP and some of the CLEP exams, students passing the EEE have shown very high levels of reading and writing ability and can appropriately receive equivalency units (again, as recommended by the American Council on Education).

The advantages of using these external programs for awarding equivalency credit are clear. The student pays all costs in test fees, the tests are careful and reliable (the campus must determine validity by deciding on appropriate credit scores), and the campus treats the credits earned as if they were transfer credits from another institution. Furthermore, studies published by AP (and unpublished studies by the EEE) have shown that students receiving credit by examination tend to take as many college units as other students, but at a more advanced level.

Nonetheless, many institutions and a large number of faculty do not have confidence in these external tests, particularly the CLEP tests. The validity of outside tests is always open to question: students may pass the test, but the test may fail to examine essential aspects of the institution's curriculum. For example, if a central goal of freshman composition is to teach the writing process or the research paper, no existing equivalency test will give scores on those skills or even attempt to measure them. ETS attempts to meet other objections about validity or standards by encouraging institutional norming of its tests. But many writing programs consider the awarding of credit by examination entirely an institutional responsibility. In such cases, the equivalency examination becomes a home-grown product.

A number of institutions, in a mistaken attempt to economize, will use scores in the high ranges of the placement test for equivalency credit. The careless reasoning behind such a policy ignores the need for a sequential curriculum, or, indeed, any curriculum for writing courses; excellent preparation to begin a study is defined as completion of the study. It is as if a student who received a perfect score on an algebra test were to be given credit for knowing calculus. This procedure makes sense only if freshman composition covers the same material as remedial composition and has the same goals. In such instances, the institution—instead of exempting those ready for freshman composition from the course—should develop a serious freshman course.

As the experience of the outside equivalency tests has shown, an equivalency test for college writing needs to be completely different from a placement test. The placement tests tend to examine sentence and word skills, modest reading skills, and ability to produce personal-experience writing with some control of the codes of expression and mechanics acceptable in the college setting. Equivalency tests, on the other hand, are based on some professional consensus of what freshman composition teaches: paragraph and essay coherence, argumentation, advanced reading skills, discovery and development of ideas, and the like. Thus, an equivalency test bases its validity not on readiness for college study but on the curriculum and goals of the freshman composition course.

The great advantage of designing a local equivalency test

comes from the curriculum discussion that must precede test development. Before a committee can define the goals of the curriculum for test purposes, those goals need to be agreed to, widely understood, and implemented in the classroom. Such a discussion is extremely valuable for any composition staff and should take place far more frequently than it normally does. But it is not easy for an institution to design an equivalency or challenge test that matches the reliability, economy, or transferability of the outside tests.

An institution could, of course, refuse to accept or offer any equivalency tests for composition. There will always be faculty to argue that "No test can evaluate what my course teaches" or that "Every student needs my course." I have even heard an apparently respected faculty member argue that students who know everything he teaches in his composition class should nonetheless be required to take his course, since they can then help the other students. Such arguments strike me as self-serving and foolish. Clearly, some students can learn writing outside our curriculum and are entitled to receive credit for what they know, so that they can move ahead at their own speed. Equivalency testing encourages advanced students and ambitious high schools to do their best; responsible institutions will support such testing. But we need to know the goals of our writing programs before we can measure whether students have achieved them.

Exit from Remedial or Freshman Composition Courses

Numbers of writing programs have developed course exit exams at both the remedial and freshman composition levels. These tests serve as final examinations for all sections of the course, and, often, students who do not pass the test will not pass the course. Although common tests for multisection courses are familiar in other fields, they are unconventional for writing programs in America. But as an understanding of the value of reliable and valid essay testing spreads among writing faculty, more and more programs are using course-wide examinations.

The common examination symbolically or even actually helps bring together the goals and standards of a multisection course. Particularly when the course is taught by many inexperienced part-timers or teaching assistants, the examination offers opportunities for coordination, communication, and peer teaching that are nowhere else available. Even senior tenured faculty will participate in the creation and scoring of such an examination, although they will rarely participate in any other activity that smacks of in-service training. Thus, the staff and the course gain substantial benefits from the mere existence of the test. Of course, the students also benefit by receiving a "staff" grade in addition to all the instructor grades they see throughout the term; for once, the instructor plays the role of coach, helping the student learn enough to pass a test external to the classroom. Even students who do not pass the test benefit from it, though they are not likely to see it that way at first. It is no favor to pass the inadequate student writer with a warm personality and tough personal luck, as some soft-hearted teachers are tempted to do. Particularly when there are other writing tests ahead, the demanding end-of-course exam at the freshman level (where extra help is likely to be available) provides a real service to the student who is not ready to move to more advanced work.

Some faculty, often the older faculty, will regard the course exit exam as an intrusion into the rights of teachers, an excess of management, even an outrage. Though I have scant sympathy for such arguments, I have seen heavy-handed and autocratic course testing that provides plenty of justification for objection. The implementation of a common exam calls for wide consultation and careful consensus building. And the results of the test should not be considered absolutely reliable. Sometimes faculty test enthusiasts lose sight of the fact that the test they have created represents only one or two short samples of first-draft writing and hence probably should not be a major or determining part of the students' grades. All the advantages of this kind of writing test fade away when examination results are misused or when an exam is inappropriate for the class.

"Rising Junior" and Upper-Division Proficiency Tests

Several state university systems, most prominently in Georgia, have given wide publicity to what they call the "rising junior" examination in writing skills. The test is based on a sensible theory that tends to work badly in practice: students should pass a statewide test of writing skill before they are allowed to proceed with many, or any, upper-division courses. Thus, the rising junior examination is normally taken at the end of the sophomore year, and it serves as a barrier to further study until it is passed. Meanwhile, other state systems, most notably in California and New York, have instituted upper-division writing proficiency requirements, which must be met before degree candidates can graduate.

These barrier tests show a clear distrust of the effectiveness of the normal curriculum. They are essentially an administrative device to validate the standards of the writing program, which, if effective, would make such a test redundant. When a large number of upper-division students have transferred lower-division work to a four-year institution, this generalized distrust of the freshman composition course is increased by the usual distrust of transfer work, particularly from community colleges or colleges perceived to have an inferior student body. For some reason, every college believes that it has higher standards than every other college (although this belief is rarely shared by outsiders), and sometimes institutions whose quality would appear (from the outside) to be questionable fiercely resist accepting outside units of any sort. This distrust of the curriculum (that of others and even of one's own) can develop into a political issue, enlisting politicians as well as academics, since it combines traditional American distrust of intellectuals with a genuine suspicion that education is not doing its job.

Aside from this problem of distrust of the curriculum and one's academic neighbors, the barrier tests pose an awkward problem of definition. Presumably, there is a level of writing ability that qualifies the student to do upper-division work, or to receive the degree, a level somewhere between that achieved at the end of freshman composition and that reached by the best students at graduation. And presumably one test will be able to discriminate reliably between those who have achieved this level and those who have not. Some kind of sophomore or upper-division writing program is thus necessary for students who fail the test; they have already received credit for freshman

composition, so they cannot be asked to repeat it. A high failure rate on the test not only confirms the dark suspicions that
gave rise to the test in the first place but also summons up a new
and quite remarkable abomination in the curriculum, the upper-
division remedial writing course (or something with a finer name,
such as intensive English or advanced writing workshop).

Since results of these barrier tests are crucial, the test becomes a major enterprise, sometimes with funding and staff that
rival the writing program. Special attention must be given to
continuous test development, to student advisement both before and after testing, and to test security and other measures
to prevent cheating. On the weekend before the test, fly-by-night
outfits are likely to appear in town with expensive materials and
cram courses in test taking. Students who have failed the test
several times become increasingly desperate and, with only the
test between them and their degrees, may resort to increasingly
desperate measures. Meanwhile, pressures to lower the standards
of the test or to provide special exemptions for an increasing
number of special cases become almost irresistible, and the test
starts to look more and more like an entrance-level minimum
competence exam (examining ability to read short passages or
to write a personal-experience essay) than a university upper-
division test of writing proficiency.

All these disadvantages await the institution that decides
to use a barrier test. Moreover, the psychometric community is
unlikely to support the test against legal challenges, since psy-
chometrists have customarily maintained that no one test is sufficiently reliable to be depended on, by itself, for a major decision about students. Furthermore, there will always be students
who have received high grades in their courses, sometimes even
in writing courses, who do not pass the test. Foreign students
pose a myriad of problems, whatever one does; graduate students (who are often required to pass the test as well) create
other kinds of problems. No inflexible policy can work, but the
world suddenly seems full of exceptions—so full that a faculty
committee is likely to argue that any exceptions will crumble
the dike.

Although proponents of the rising junior test argue that it
protects institutional standards and is more humane than an

exit barrier test for the degree (since it comes relatively early in a student's course of study), I do not see much difference between the two kinds of tests; I also have serious doubts about the economic and educational soundness of this kind of examination. Since it is a barrier test, it must meet the highest psychometric standards of validity and reliability; litigious students are particularly likely to appeal failing grades on this test because the stakes are very high and the courts are more sympathetic to the apparent withholding of "property rights" to a degree than they are to other, more internal, academic appeals. If the same funding and energy required for a responsible rising junior test were put into freshman placement testing and writing programs, the test would be unnecessary, and the education provided the students would be enhanced. If institutional standards need further protection, I would rather see a required upper-division writing course than a barrier test outside the curriculum.

Either a rising junior or an upper-division writing test as a barrier for graduation poses major problems for any institution, problems that can be avoided if the requirement is handled through an instructional program. On the other hand, a required upper-division writing course provides an appropriate curriculum to achieve the desired goal. Such a course does call for careful coordination, supervision, and distribution of teaching responsibilities; it cannot be left to the English department, though normally a composition specialist will coordinate the course. The English department cannot become alone responsible for university writing quality, nor can it take on the onus of denying degrees to students approved by everyone else; such a procedure allows the rest of the faculty (whose lack of concern for student writing has spurred the demand for proficiency certification) free to continue business as usual. But if key faculty in each school or department can become committed to the upper-division writing course, the writing requirement becomes part of the curriculum (perhaps a general education requirement) and part of what the university stands for. If an examination is needed, a high-level equivalency test could be prepared for those students who are unusually capable and wish to "challenge" the course requirement.

A bona fide upper-division required writing program fosters a series of high-quality seminars in writing for different departmental majors, promotes concern throughout the university for improving student writing, and leads to a high-quality challenge test for those few students who can demonstrate they do not need the course. Special support services for the weak students can be provided through the learning center, without singling out and grouping these students. Although such a program appears more costly than a minimum proficiency test, it provides important benefits for the money, instead of a university-size headache. Instead of putting major effort and money into an embarrassingly low-level test, with its attendant embarrassing upper-division remedial writing course, the university can put its resources into a high-quality upper-division writing program and a small, high-quality challenge test. Those teaching and those taking the required course will have no incentive to debase it (as is unfortunately the case with remedial work); it will in fact seem more like a senior honors seminar than a freshman composition class, and students as well as faculty will bring inventiveness and interest to it.

"Value-Added" Testing and Program Evaluation

In "value-added" testing and program evaluation, an attempt is made to measure the direct gain from a particular curriculum. Value-added testing is the cruder of these concepts; it comes from the world of commerce, most directly from the European value-added tax on goods. Thus, raw rubber has a certain value when it reaches the tire plant, but much more value after it has been turned into tires; that added value can be identified, measured, and taxed. For both of these kinds of assessment, "gain scores" from parallel tests usually must be obtained. Improved scores on the posttests show that the program, or the individual, is doing what should be done. Outcomes assessment is the guiding term, and a certain kind of behaviorism is the underlying psychological theory.

The concept has a certain superficial and political appeal, in particular to those for whom commercial metaphors are a dominant means of perceiving reality. Behaviorism makes a powerful claim: If education has brought about changes of any sort, as every educator asserts, then those changes should appear in measurable behaviors that can be tested. If a teacher or an entire discipline cannot come up with measures that produce results, either no real change has taken place or the faculty are unclear about instructional goals and therefore cannot tell whether the goals have been reached. Arguments about gains that are qualitative rather than quantitative, or about insensitive measuring tools, are dismissed as smoke screens, rather in the same tone that Skinner used in dismissing the concepts of freedom and dignity in his famous book. In addition, for once, this measurement concept favors the *less* privileged students and institutions, since those who begin at a very low point are most likely to show gain scores on tests. Selective institutions, on the other hand, are hard pressed to come up with measurement devices that readily and economically show measurable gains for students already functioning at high cognitive and skill levels. Such institutions are no longer spared these demands; indeed, their high tuition spurs demands for assessment to prove that the education they offer is worth the price. Meanwhile, of course, the liberal arts suffer badly in comparison with vocational and technical training, which lend themselves to the concept of learning as simple accrual of skill and information.

Unfortunately for the behaviorist perspective, we have yet to come up with writing tests that are sensitive enough to be used as pre/post measures to quantify the value added to individual writing skill (out of a lifetime of language use) by a single writing course. Despite great gains in reliability for holistic scoring over the last twenty-five years, there is still only slim evidence that a direct writing measure (such as an essay test) can yield sufficiently precise data to provide clear gain scores. Of the more than five hundred studies that met George Hillocks's (1986) criteria for inclusion in his literature review, only sixty could be included in his meta-analyses, and few of them tested anything more elaborate than sentence skills.

Pre/post testing therefore puts a premium on low-level skills that can be easily examined through multiple-choice tests and readily improved by short-term learning or drill. But while

such testing may work in some fields, it is particularly danger-
ous in writing and other liberal arts fields, where outcomes are
complex and not necessarily immediately manifest. Benjamin
Bloom, in his educational taxonomy, warns against simplified
testing, which often works in opposition to the important goals
of education; he warns, for example, that an emphasis on knowledge about literature (which can be readily tested) can destroy
the love of literature, which is far more important but much
more difficult to assess (Bloom and others, 1971).

In theory, and occasionally in practice, it is possible to
test for advances in even very complicated skills, such as a
writer's ability to use sources to support rather than substitute
for ideas, or the ability to blend detail and generalization in
order to create a convincing argument. But such tests would require substantial writing and careful scoring of that writing; despite the effort and expense, they still might not yield statistically
significant data, even in cases where every teacher and student
knows that important gains have occurred. In most cases, unfortunately, pre/post testing does not anticipate such complicated
assessment. We are much more likely to see multiple-choice tests
of footnote format or detail clusters ("Which of the following
details does not fit with the rest?").

It is important to notice the crucial difference between
equivalency testing and pre/post testing. The equivalency test is
concerned only with achieved goals and criteria and does not attempt to give pretests. It can thus measure student writing and
reading achievement without regard for how, when, or where
this achievement occurred. Most equivalency tests, in fact, are
considerably more demanding than final exams in a course,
since they must take pains not to give course credit to the mar-
ginal student. By definition, the equivalency test population is
made up of atypical students with special interest in the field.
It would be absurd to give an equivalency test to those beginning a course of study, for virtually everyone would do very
badly; the purely administrative function of the exercise would
be so apparent that many students, frustrated by a difficult examination on material they have not yet studied, would not take
the test seriously. But in value-added testing and much program

evaluation, every student must be given a pretest, so that pre-test scores can be compared with posttest scores. All the pressures on equivalency tests urge high standards to challenge the exceptional student; all the pressures on value-added tests urge low standards, so that every student can participate and show some gain.

A generation ago, a similar idea came and disappeared with unusual speed. Education through "behavioral objectives" called for detailed statements of goals for instruction (for example, "90 percent of my students will spell correctly 90 percent of the words on this list") and frequent testing to see whether the goals have been met. The goals, however, had to be "behavioral"—that is, readily observable and measurable. The hard-headed Skinnerians behind the movement declared that less obvious gains, such as attitude changes or general improvement in cognitive ability, would appear as behaviors. Despite its simple-mindedness, the concept did force teachers to state what they were trying to do and how they would measure success. Certainly, such a process is valuable for any teacher. But a first-grade teacher, delighted with the concept, unwittingly pointed out its serious deficiency when I asked her how she could write behavioral objectives for much of what (in my naivete) I took to be the first-grade curriculum: story telling, poetry, art, or music appreciation. "No problem," she told me, cheerfully. "We just don't teach those things anymore." At the university level, a reluctant scholar required to write behavioral objectives for his upper-division Shakespeare course (during the heights of the fad) responded with appropriate cynicism. His goal for *Macbeth*, he wrote, was that 90 percent of his students, 90 percent of the time, would not kill a king.

Nonetheless, behaviorism, with its powerful appeal, cannot be ignored when it is in fashion. Some institutions or English departments will have to come up with assessments (which need not be the same as tests) that purport to measure the value added to a student by a composition course or program. If such a procedure becomes necessary, responsible academic institutions should take the following steps:

1. Create, through extensive consultation and discussion, a careful set of clearly defined goals for the course or program.
2. Develop from these goals a set of criteria for a measurement device, which need not—indeed, should not—be only a multiple-choice test.
3. Select or create one or more measurement devices that will provide valid and reliable measurement of those developed criteria.
4. Solicit sufficient funds and other support to administer the measurement device (which could include portfolios or other extended activities as well as timed tests).
5. Keep careful statistical and other records of all pretest and posttest scores and of all academic and demographic data for use by the statisticians who need to prepare the evaluation documents.
6. Maintain final editorial control of the evaluation document, so that the goals and criteria stated in that document represent those agreed on by the faculty rather than those envisioned by the statistical consultants.

Such a sophisticated procedure and measurement device may still not produce the required data, but it will have a positive effect on instruction and therefore is worth the doing whatever the result.

The academic community always has a difficult time responding to behaviorist demands by trustees, legislators, and the Skinnerian educationists who provide them with advice. Sometimes, as in Missouri and California in 1987, a populist governor or legislator will seize upon simplified testing as a way of purporting to help students get their money's worth from colleges and college professors with scant interest in teaching. The politician's claim that he is defending student interests is often not taken seriously by academics, who see only an outsider pressing for a debasement of the curriculum by means of shoddy tests; few academics are willing to debate the issue. But such a politically unwise stance merely confirms the general impression that the politician is on to something important and that the recalcitrant institutions and professors are covering up their inability to educate students. A much wiser approach would be to accept the concept that complex subjects such as a writing course do indeed add value to students (how can we argue or allow anyone to argue otherwise?) but to decline to accept the behaviorist definition of value or the simplistic measurement devices that are usually proposed. We should in good faith join in the attempt to come up with sophisticated and appropriate ways of measuring writing ability, since such assessment will help, not hurt, us. But we do need to point out to the politicians that the research involved is expensive and the results uncertain; they may suddenly be reluctant to pursue their agenda when they see how much it may cost. Institutions at risk of such well-motivated intrusion should know that a responsible assessment program in place is the surest defense against pressure for inappropriate testing.

As I argue in Chapter Five, measurement is a useful, even necessary, part of writing instruction. But pre/post testing without substantial funding and full-scale faculty involvement is a dangerously reductive idea for education, one that asks testing to carry much more responsibility than it can shoulder and one that imperils the liberal arts. It does, however, have the particular advantage of requiring faculty to review the goals of instruction and to seek ways of assessing degrees of achievement of those goals. That advantage is likely to remain long after the particular testing devices have been discarded.

Some readers may feel that this chapter, with its focus on testing programs, has already dealt sufficiently with administrative issues in relation to writing programs, the subject of the next several chapters. In one sense, it may have, since so much administrative time these days is devoted to placement and certification problems. But a college or university administration must concern itself with much more than the testing aspect of the writing program if the campus climate for writing is to be a positive one, encouraging writing in all parts of the campus and fostering writing for discovery, critical thinking, and creativity.

The campus writing program involves teachers and students in classes, working within a structured set of courses and support services, directed by a WPA, in a campus context of students and faculty with goals in part directed by the institution. We now turn to these larger issues.

Chapter 7

Establishing an Effective
Writing Program on Campus

College and university writing programs usually develop organically as needs appear; they are not so much planned or organized as inherited and casually coordinated. As I have said in earlier chapters, on most campuses the separate activities and courses relating to composition are not usually even seen as a writing program, nor are they normally administered in an orderly way. For example, one campus I visited had four separate writing tutorial programs (in the learning center, the Educational Opportunity Program, the English department, and the counseling center), all designed to assist the same student population: underprivileged freshmen. Meanwhile, upper-division students with writing problems had nowhere to turn for assistance, and even regular freshmen with special difficulties were left out in the cold. None of the four tutorial programs (which competed heavily for resources) was well funded or well directed. Although the same resources could have been used to establish a first-rate single facility that could have met wider needs, no one on campus was in a position to notice the problem and bring about this change.

Administrative Oversight

This lack of organization, we might say optimistically, expresses the wide-ranging nature of college writing; that is, since

136

writing underlies almost all the learning that takes place at the institution, instruction and support may turn up almost everywhere. But disorganization has only limited value. Without administrative oversight of the writing program as a whole, some important needs are likely to be ignored while others may be met partially in several different locations under different auspices. Since resources tend to be limited and writing needs are so large, it makes good sense to focus and manage the program under a general plan. Such organization requires a sense of the writing program as a whole and of its relationship to the philosophy and organization of the college.

Before the writing program can be seen as a whole, someone in the institution must have responsibility for the whole program. In Chapter One, I argued for a strong writing program administrator (WPA); to function effectively, however, even a strong WPA usually needs a powerful ally in the administrative structure—someone in central administration with direct responsibility for writing. Most colleges and universities at present have no office or person charged with such responsibility, although most administrators believe that someone else is taking care of the job. The university administration is likely to feel that all writing issues are the proper business of the English department and that the English chair is naturally assuming responsibility for them. However, the English chair may pay only passing attention to the composition course (or delegate that responsibility to a WPA) and normally feels little concern for the rest of the writing program, which clearly is a domain beyond the department. On some campuses—as those of us who are asked to appraise university composition programs have found— no one is even aware of all the components of the program.

A few universities have sought to solve this organizational problem by appointing a Dean of Writing, or some similar title. The idea does not seem to have caught on, however, since a new administrative title outside the usual patterns of funding and lines of responsibility inevitably winds up outside the internal power structure. The idea that writing is so separate from the rest of the curriculum that it should have its own office also appears to relieve others of their responsibilities; if the Dean of

Writing is doing the job, why should the psychology department be concerned about the writing abilities of its majors, or the learning center worry about writing across the curriculum? Furthermore, a separate office suggests a separate discipline, rather than an underlying one; it is hard to imagine a Dean of Reading or a Dean of Listening, for instance, important as those underemphasized concerns may be for the learning of students.

A few other campuses have developed campus-wide faculty committees on writing, which (when the committee chair happens to be energetic and willing to devote extra time) can have a strong influence on the organization of the writing program. But such committees generally lack the institutional memory of an administrative office, depend for their power on the good will of the faculty and administration, and vary widely from year to year in their effectiveness.

The most effective plan is often the simplest: an existing office inside the power structure of the university should assume administrative responsibility for the entire writing program, in support of the WPA. On many campuses, the office of the Dean of Instruction, or Undergraduate Studies, or Academic Programs would be appropriate; on one campus with which I am familiar, the provost is the key line administrator who signs major documents. Whatever the office or individual appropriate to a particular campus, the administrator should be assigned to review, support, and report on the writing program as a whole. This administrator would depend heavily on the work of the faculty and staff coordinating aspects of the program, most particularly a strong WPA, but would be able to focus attention and resources on the program from an institutional perspective. This administrative task is far from minor, since whoever is assigned to the task must be aware of the wide-ranging and underlying importance of the complex enterprise.

Surely, the first step for an administration seeking to order and improve its campus climate for writing would be a systematic assessment of the writing program as it presently exists. Some guidance for such a self-study is available in the materials published by the two federally funded projects described in Chapter Two, but the most practical help is provided by the Council of Writing Program Administrators, which, supported in part by the Exxon Foundation, has been offering low-cost writing program evaluation to campuses for some years. Even campuses unwilling to follow through with outside evaluations can use the council's self-study guide as a way to see clearly the strengths and weaknesses of their present program—or, indeed, to see the various campus writing services, tests, and curricula as a program. (For the 1988 version of the council's guidelines for self-study to precede a writing program evaluation, see Resource B at the back of this book.) Outside visitors, and their subsequent reports, cannot be equated with empirical program evaluations, but they can be powerful agents for clear perception and change.

Philosophy and Goals

Academic programs, like people, most fully articulate their goals by their behavior, not by their statements. Nonetheless, a statement of the philosophy and goals of the writing program can be a valuable document. Its preparation forces each segment of the program to define what it is doing and why and to connect its particular goals with institutional goals. Thus, the preparation and the adoption of such a document logically follow an institutional self-assessment. How does each program segment define "writing"? What is it seeking to accomplish? What does it need in order to accomplish these goals more effectively? After much discussion, these statements should cohere in some way and should be sequential in some way, leading to the overall institutional goals statement. The process, no doubt, will be more valuable than the product, since review of the document requires people to hear what their colleagues are saying. But the product will also be important for developing the writing program, since it establishes the philosophical context within which the program must operate.

Once the campus has before it a clear statement of the philosophy and goals of its writing program, and an assessment of its present strengths and weaknesses, and once the institution has decided to focus responsibility for that program, it is in a position to review the way it is organized to meet the goals it has set. The rest of this chapter will look at the organizational issues that most affect the campus climate for writing.

Developing a Freshman Writing Program

Placement

Two kinds of colleges often resist entry placement of students in writing classes: elite institutions, which would like to believe that demanding entrance requirements establish the writing competence of all freshmen, and open-enrollment institutions, which often imagine that placement will stereotype or discourage those with weak preparation. In addition, some colleges with homogeneous student bodies believe that placement is a waste of time and money, since there are few differences among entering students. Meanwhile, many faculty and administrators believe that placement of students into remedial instruction on campus somehow damages the quality and seriousness of their institution.

As I argued in the previous chapter, I am unconvinced by these arguments, as are the vast majority of American colleges, which give placement tests of one sort or another. Even highly selective colleges enroll at least three kinds of students who are disadvantaged in freshman composition and who need support if they are to succeed: (1) "special admit" students without the social, economic, or educational advantages of the rest of the student body; (2) students with special talents in sports or science or the arts but primitive writing ability; and (3) certain regular "good" students who have learned to follow rules dutifully without thinking about or taking responsibility for what they are saying. At the other end of the line of privilege, many open-enrollment institutions experimented in the 1960s with "self-placement": they would offer a range of writing courses, including remedial work, but would rely on students' judgment to select the appropriate level of work. An unpublished study by one of my graduate students compared this self-placement by entering students at seven open-enrollment community colleges in California with scores achieved by those same students on placement tests; there was only a random correlation between writing ability as measured by these tests and the decision to enroll in regular or remedial reading courses. In follow-up interviews, the graduate student collected enough information to conclude that the self-placement resulted more from the students' general level of self-confidence than from self-perception of writing ability.

Administrators' statements about placement of students often differ from what the teachers of writing classes have to say. Administrators may say that placement is not needed, for various reasons, or that voluntary placement by student choice is effective, but the teachers of freshmen are likely to tell us (perhaps only in private) that the wide range of student abilities in their classes makes it extremely difficult for them to pay attention to the needs of all their students.

When there is no placement of students in the freshman composition course, and hence no remedial program, instructors are faced with a problem for which there is no good solution: whose needs to focus on? Typically, a class under these conditions will contain a group of well-prepared students ready for the challenge of demanding reading and writing assignments and another group with only the most rudimentary reading and writing ability. Some teachers will teach to the advanced group, demanding much and receiving the reward of seeing great improvement from students who have often been neglected by the schools; these teachers will see the weak students drop out or fail, since, no matter how much help they may receive, the work required is simply too advanced for them. Other teachers will not bother to challenge the top group and will focus their attention on the neediest ones in the class. Still other teachers will break the class into different groups working at different levels, a pedagogical feat beyond the capacity (and available time) of most of the young teachers who are employed at small wages to handle the course.

The accumulated experience of most American colleges suggests that several levels of composition instruction are necessary at almost all institutions, and that some form of mandatory (not voluntary) student advisement and placement is needed to assist students in finding appropriate courses. Furthermore, placement testing does not discourage students; most entering students regard such testing (when it is not associated with admissions decisions) as supportive and helpful—a form of institutional "caring" that is appreciated. Of course, the placement testing must be appropriate and sensible (see Chapter Six); and—since no test is wholly reliable—there must be an opportunity during the first week of classes for some shifting of those misplaced by the test.

Remedial Programs

The decisions to be made about entry-level writing placement are fundamental to the purpose of the institution and hence require substantial discussion at the institutional level. The questions follow in this sequence:

1. Is there enough range of skills among entering freshmen to call for one or more "remedial" composition classes?
2. If so, what shall be the curriculum and goals of the remedial program and who shall teach it? Should this program offer graduation credit and how shall it be funded?
3. After there is a clear sense of the goals of the remedial program and the goals of freshman composition, what kind of placement device should be used and how?

The advantages of placement testing followed by sensitive mandatory placement in a planned curriculum are great. The weakest students will receive an appropriate curriculum for their needs and sufficient attention so that they will have a fair chance of success when they are admitted into the regular composition course. Data collected by the California State University and by the Department of Higher Education in New Jersey have shown that the persistence rate of low-scoring students can be improved substantially by such attention. There is no point in admitting students with weak preparation and offering them little chance to succeed; as with colleges proud of their athletic success, colleges with special recruiting programs for underprepared or unconventionally prepared students should be asked to publish completion rates, not merely recruiting data.

But the principal beneficiaries of a remedial program are not the weak students, even though their success rates will improve dramatically with sensitive placement testing, instruction, and support. The examples in the previous chapter (in the section on placement) show that such a program benefits the entire curriculum. The level of instruction in the freshman writing course can now be sufficiently high so that it can demand the complex reading, advanced thinking, and developed writing that alone argue for its place in the required college curriculum. The best students can now be challenged by the course instead of bored by it, and the best teachers can be induced to teach the course, since it has substance and quality. The faculty are not faced with the impossible choice of whom to neglect in the class, since those not ready for it are developing elsewhere. Thus, the entire college stands to benefit from an appropriate remedial program, since it leads directly to a more effective freshman composition course and, hence, a better-prepared student body.

Freshman Composition

Almost all American campuses have a well-established freshman composition program, one that has evolved in response to the needs of the particular student body and the interests of the faculty. I need not repeat here the cautions and advice to teachers given in earlier chapters. But we should pause to examine a few additional administrative issues that require discussion and decision. I have just looked at the most important of these, for most campuses: the establishment of an appropriate remedial program, which then allows freshman composition to focus on careful reading, critical thinking, and college-level writing. But many other issues remain, such as the following:

Level of Standardization. On some campuses, every section of freshman composition is its own separate course; the instructor has total autonomy to choose texts, syllabus, approaches, goals, and standards. On other campuses, all or most of these matters are standardized, decided either by a powerful WPA or an equally powerful committee. I have problems with both extremes, uneasy about the perils of anarchy as well as of dictatorship, and find myself most comfortable somewhere in the middle. It makes sense to have staff agreement on such matters as the particular dictionary and handbook to be required, the general amount and kind of reading and writing to be assigned, and the course standards and goals. But, given the lack of agreement about most other matters, the staff should have freedom to experiment with particular texts and assignments (perhaps within some agreed limits) and to discover the most appropriate approach for their own teaching styles. Most faculty prefer to be left alone, and most faculty use that freedom wisely; but the institution and the students need to be protected from classes that depart from agreed policy.

Exit Examinations. Some freshman composition programs require every student in every section to take and pass a common examination in order to pass the class. Such a requirement adds credibility to the course and provides support to the faculty concerned about maintaining high standards. But some faculty will find such a test both unnecessary and intrusive.

Length and Sequence. The traditional two-semester sequence for freshman composition has been weakened by the wide variety of academic calendars now in use and by a certain lack of enthusiasm in its defense. The traditional "ownership" of the composition sequence by the English department has also been challenged by writing-across-the-curriculum programs. The first-term freshman composition course remains firmly ensconced, but the second and later courses can no longer be considered beyond question. In various ways, composition courses have been moved from their more traditional locations, to reinforce the importance of writing throughout the university and throughout all years of study.

Developing Writing-Across-the-Curriculum Courses

For some campuses, writing is a mechanical requirement to be "gotten out of the way," as some well-meaning academic advisers will put it, in the freshman year. Then, after the rest of general education is also gotten out of the way, the student can get down to serious business, such as learning psychology or accounting. On other campuses, writing and writing courses continue throughout the student's education, as a fundamental learning and thinking skill. The first of these two patterns is by far more usual in America. The customary vocational and disciplinary pressures on campus curricula—combined with a national culture in which reading and writing often seem peripheral to what really matters—will push writing aside unless deliberate efforts are made to keep it at the center. A campus that wants writing to be more than something to be gotten out of the way will need to plan to keep writing in the way. Specifically, it must place students appropriately into whatever levels of the freshman writing program need to be established; demand a high level of performance from the students completing the freshman requirement; remain aware that some students will require more time than others to reach that level; provide substantial support programs to all freshmen, so that most of them will be able to succeed; and enforce genuine writing requirements beyond the freshman course. The most substantial way to pursue this last goal has become known as "writing across the curriculum"—that is, demonstrating that writing is much more than a narrow concern of the English department.

Sophomore Writing Courses

Many colleges and universities have reached the conclusion that the freshman program is not enough. Some of these institutions have replaced the usual two terms of freshman composition with one term of freshman composition and one term of sophomore writing. The second course calls for a more advanced curriculum: a focus on writing the research paper, perhaps, or faculty seminars in special topics, or such general education topics as multicultural perspectives. An inventive approach to the course will open the teaching to faculty from all departments, not only from English, and combine it with a faculty development program in writing across the curriculum. Whatever arrangement is most appropriate for the campus and the student body, the new message of a sophomore writing requirement is clear: Writing is a means of learning beyond the freshman year.

Upper-Division Writing Programs

A campus that is prepared to plan a writing program, rather than passively watch one emerge out of reaction to events, can develop upper-division writing courses that fit with its general education program and enhance the education of all its students. Such writing courses ought to involve faculty from all disciplines, working together under coordination from a professional in the field of writing. The courses must keep the emphasis on writing, rather than on the field of study, even though the reading material will vary from discipline to discipline. One faculty senate, for example, has specified that upper-division general education writing courses must meet the following conditions: (1) a minimum of 6,000 words of writing, exclusive of required revisions, in a minimum of six separate papers; (2) instruction in the writing of analytical and research papers; (3) instruction in the writing of summaries and precis; (4) participation in the university-wide common examination given each term in all sections of the upper-division writing program. While different campuses will adopt different specifications, some such firm central direction is needed if an upper-division writing program is to get established at all.

The benefits of an upper-division writing program are many, going beyond the message that writing is necessary past the freshman level. Since faculty from all disciplines will necessarily be involved in teaching, they form a natural constituency for a writing-across-the-curriculum faculty development program, with all of its positive influence. As these faculty participate in both the teach'ng and the learning that a writing course demands, they naturally increase the quantity and quality of writing they require in classes in their own disciplines, thus carrying out in practice the truism that every teacher needs to support the use of writing as a means of learning. (See Gere, 1985b, for an outstanding collection of essays on writing across the curriculum, and Walvoord, 1986, for a fine text.) Meanwhile, the freshman and sophomore writing courses gain new seriousness because they prepare students for advanced required courses. Finally, when graduates of such a curriculum are asked to write on the job or in professional school, as most of them will be, they find it a customary and practiced thing to do. Such graduates are the beneficiaries of a planned college writing program which keeps them from believing that writing should be gotten out of the way as soon as possible.

A number of policy questions need to be resolved in order to allow for the positive situation I have just described. If the campus has at present no writing program beyond the freshman level, it is likely to turn to the English department to plan and staff new courses. The English department will argue that its literature major is now threatened by its heavy composition teaching burden and that it cannot handle more service courses for the university. Where administrative energies are weak, the effort stops at this point. For this effort to go forward, administrators might appoint an all-campus committee to make receptive faculty in all departments aware of the importance of developing expanded writing programs. An inventive institution can find support for such an initiative. Many existing programs have begun with an outside grant to bring about a full writing program, and many public foundations (for example, the National Endowment for the Humanities) and private ones (the Lilly Endowment, the Bush Foundation) have made substantial funding available for such purposes. English departments, which normally react negatively to proposals that place all responsibility for student writing on their shoulders, are often willing, even eager, to provide leadership in a serious campus-wide effort to improve student writing.

The best resource for those implementing a course or a program in writing across the curriculum is the review essay by James Kinneavy in *Teaching Composition* (Tate, 1987, pp. 353–377). This essay lists the standard sources of research, texts, and model programs; it also sets out some of the issues and effects associated with the programs. Kinneavy's conclusion, that "the jury is out" on the results, does not keep him from asserting that "at the present, the promise seems most favorable—writing across the curriculum may be the best academic response to the literacy crisis in English-speaking countries, though it cannot be a total response" (p. 377).

Work Load in Writing-Across-the-Curriculum Programs

One of the first problems that will emerge, after a serious effort is under way to involve all departments in the teaching of writing at all levels, is work load. A history faculty member on my campus argues that he works twice as many hours to teach a social science expository writing class as he does to teach a history class. Despite much talk about involving students in their own learning, much college teaching still goes on in the old style. Teachers lecture from familiar or even innovative notes, and the students show that they have memorized what the teacher has said by passing multiple-choice tests. Such a comfortable pattern, which demands little from teacher or student, is obviously inappropriate for any writing class (though numbers of teachers do attempt to use it). Faculty who might want to become involved in the writing program are legitimately concerned about doubling their work load with a different pedagogy and constant interaction with students.

Two kinds of responses are necessary if these (often hidden) work-load issues are not to undermine all attempts to develop a writing program. The first is simple: writing classes should be held to no more than twenty students. To cover the funding for these smaller writing classes, public universities as well as elite private colleges can simply expand the size of classes taught by the lecture/multiple-choice-test method. Since student conferences and individualized reading of papers, both in draft and in final form, are involved in the teaching of writing courses, a reasonable student load is essential if faculty outside the English department (and the tenured English faculty as well) are to be induced to teach them.

I say this work-load issue is simple not because the required financial shifting of priorities is easy to accomplish but because there is not much room for debate about the issue. Just as in our private lives we determine our real priorities by what we spend our money on (whatever we may pretend), so does a university. If the university administration pretends that writing courses are a high priority but refuses to fund the small classes necessary to do the job, there is not much point in proceeding further. Unless the funding to offer the program is available, at least potentially, all-campus writing committees and everything they attempt to accomplish are a waste of time and effort.

The second response to the work-load issue is to establish a writing-across-the-curriculum faculty development program to help faculty use writing more effectively as part of teaching. Most faculty outside the field of English have had no experience with writing courses beyond the freshman composition course they took as students and hence know nothing about the advances in knowledge and pedagogy that have occurred in the field. They often think that the teaching of writing means only endless red-marking of student writing products, with an emphasis on mechanics. They need to learn about ways of teaching the writing process, of the intellectual excitement present in good writing classes, of the relation of reading to writing, of ways of using peer response to expand the audience for writing beyond themselves. A writing program is empty unless it takes seriously the need to educate the faculty as well as the students.

Although such a faculty development program is essential, it need not be expensive. Some campuses (such as my own) simply make the direction of such a seminar part of a writing specialist's teaching load and systematically recruit faculty to take the seminar. Other campuses use more elaborate (and expensive) formats, with guest lecturers and honoraria for the faculty participants. Whatever plan is used, some kind of systematic and collegial seminar is necessary for a writing program to take hold. The literature on faculty development, and on writing across the curriculum, is rich with examples of procedures and benefits. When this kind of faculty development is integrated naturally into the overall campus writing program, the campus climate for writing becomes exceedingly healthy.

Related Programs and Services

Whoever is responsible for administering the writing program needs to see it as a whole, including related programs and services such as writing centers, tutoring services, counseling centers, reading labs, library workshops, learning centers, English as a Second Language (ESL) programs, educational opportunity programs, and computer writing labs. Each of these services may be attending to its own clientele and goals without reference to the rest of the writing program, or may even be in conflict with other parts of the program; at the same time, the best writing instruction on campus may be going on in the basements and out-of-the-way nooks where these services normally find grudging space. Intelligent administration will both foster these programs and restrict duplication or competition, a task much easier to state than to do.

Several of these services have expanded into specialties of their own, with professional organizations and journals, and so have claims to be considered an integral part of any collegiate institution. For example, the National Writing Centers Association is a designated assembly of the National Council of Teachers of English and publishes the *Writing Center Journal.* The professionals who make their careers in writing centers see them as much more than a campus "fix-it shop" or "comma clinic." In a seminal article on "The Idea of a Writing Center," Stephen North (1984) argues for the importance of the center as a place where serious talk about writing and the writing process leads to significant learning: "Writing centers are simply one manifestation—polished and highly visible—of a dialogue about writing that is central to higher education" (p. 440). These centers, in North's view, can develop into "centers of consciousness about writing on campuses, a kind of physical locus for the ideas and ideals of college or university or high school commitment to writing" (p. 446). The same metaphor of centrality dominates Irene Clark's (1985) *Writing in the Center.* She notes, for example, that "Teaching in a Writing Center is now as important as teaching in a traditional classroom" (p. v). Carol Haviland (1985) has argued that the writing center should take the lead in "moving writing instruction out of the center and into courses across the curriculum" (p. 25). Perhaps a thriving writing center could be the location for all tutoring or remedial programs, as well as a focus for writing across the curriculum, visiting poets, and writing research, as proponents have argued. But other programs on campus will be ready to see such a move as an encroachment on their areas or budgets, perhaps even an attack on special minority support services or some departmental prerogatives.

The same issues apply to ESL, a thriving discipline of its own, with an uncertain relation to university and college writing programs. Typically, ESL programs will focus on intensive listening, speaking, and reading, with writing as a way to test those skills; the heavy grammar emphasis of such programs often devalues writing as discovery and critical thinking. But these programs cannot do everything at once, and they often see themselves in conflict with the regular writing program, which has little understanding of the language problems faced by students from other language cultures.

The problems relating to writing support services are never simple. For example, the advent of word processing and text-editing software has moved the computer center into the writing business, sometimes despite itself. Early enthusiasm that the new technology would somehow transform and elevate all student writing has since given way to some hard realities: ease of production of writing does not necessarily lead to better prose; and all kinds of new pedagogical problems, and possibilities, are now before us. Several publishers of English handbooks provide word processing software, including spelling checkers, for about the cost of a standard textbook. Yet, where many students become accustomed to using university computers for writing, the facilities rapidly become inadequate, which leads to other kinds of problems. Yesterday's solutions, typically enough, create today's problems, calling for tomorrow's proposed solutions.

Any attempt to understand and harmonize the various support services on a campus will be greeted with some suspicion, but should lead to wiser use of available resources. At the very least, some communication among the competing programs is bound to occur, a great advance from the present situation on most campuses.

Policies

Definition of Entering-Level Writing Ability

A statement prepared by the college, with examples, about the reading and writing ability expected of entering students, those who are ready to begin the regular composition program, will be valuable for schools preparing students for college and, particularly, for the establishment or review of a remedial program.

One way to help focus the remedial program is to develop, update, and publicize a clear statement of goals for the course, which should, of course, relate directly to the institution's definition of entering-level writing ability. Those who write this document will have to be familiar with both the remedial program, if there is one, and the regular freshman composition course. What kinds of reading ability are called for? Which writing skills are assumed, and which are taught? If the regular composition program requires students to be able to analyze poetry or to read complex social science prose with comprehension, the college should say so and should define students without such reading skill as remedial. Does the regular course assume an ability to write coherent and developed paragraphs, or is that part of what is taught? What about dictionary and library experience? What is the role of spelling and punctuation? Laboratory reports? Research?

Preparation of a policy statement is likely to reveal inconsistencies in practice. The regular composition course may begin with the writing of clear, coherent paragraphs, assuming that students already understand sentence structure, whereas the remedial course may have ignored sentence structure and concentrated on paragraph coherence. Or perhaps the regular course assumes that students know how to write coherent essays, whereas the remedial program never gets beyond sentence structure. Again, typically, remedial writing courses ignore severe reading problems to focus on drill in writing mechanics; success in the regular course may, however, depend on reading skill more than on correctness.

Clear definitions do not imply rigidity. The Harvard entrance requirements at the turn of the century, to take the most familiar example of rigidity, listed the precise books to be read in the schools (and, to some extent, how they were to be read) and were allowed to impose a kind of chill on the high school curriculum. But it is not arrogant or rigid to state the *kind* of reading material that students are expected to be able to read or the *kind* of writing they should be able to perform at college entrance. Such statements do need to reflect reality, not abstract theory, and they need to be sensitive to both the students and the schools. When they are careful and realistic, they provide major support to the schools and a clear guide to the remedial program.

Credit for Remedial Work

The inevitable argument about offering college credit for remedial work sometimes becomes so consuming that the compelling benefits of the program get lost in the discussion. No matter how this vexed argument is settled—and I am convinced that there is no really good way to settle it—it should be kept in its place as a bureaucratic detail.

Those who argue that remedial work should not receive college credit generally assume that there is a common and ascertainable definition of what that remedial work consists of and that it should have been taught elsewhere. While that assumption about the meaning of remedial writing is not well founded (since each college will define the concept in relation to its own students and its own curriculum), the quantitative argument is hard to dispute: students who earn college credit for elementary work will take fewer credits in advanced work, and hence receive a less advanced education. On the other hand, those who believe that remedial work should receive college credit argue that college studies demand college credit, and they point to foreign language, physical education, art, and music for parallel examples. American colleges and universities, they will argue, are not like European ones, which certify levels of achievement by examination; our institutions attempt to bring each student as far as the student can go in the time available for study.

We must simply accept the fact that there are powerful, flawed, and value-laden arguments on both sides of the issue. The decision will ultimately be made on political grounds, not according to rational argument. If the institution is concerned about the quality of the freshman writing program and the needs of its entering students, it will find a way to accommodate the conflicting arguments in a practical solution; with good will, there are many ways to live with the problem. Unhappily, some of the inherited solutions turn out to be cynical. For example, some institutions solve the problem by refusing college credit and charging additional fees for remedial work; one must wonder why such institutions bother to admit students who need extra help if that help is defined as unrewarding and made prohibitively expensive. One large midwestern university used to consider its enormous freshman composition program virtually a practical wing of the admissions office. The battalion of graduate students teaching the admitted freshmen were given the grim duty of failing those they judged unable to complete college work, who could then be dismissed. On the other hand, institutions more sensitive to student and societal needs have found ways to fund and to award special kinds of credit units for remedial and developmental work, which might require extensive time from some admitted students. Other colleges have found ways to attach units to the regular composition course for special tutoring or other support work. Yet another solution has its comic side. To avoid the appearance of awarding graduation credit for something intended as remedial work, some colleges nonetheless do so by inflating course descriptions and numbers. My favorite example is the remedial course that one California institution labeled English 1000, Advanced Writing Workshop.

The decisions that are made about remedial credit and funding demonstrate the institution's commitment not only to

pus. But here I am also considering an educational problem that most college teachers face: how to help perfectly honest students gain control over the information and opinions they collect in relation to the papers they are writing. Even competent upper-division students are normally bewildered when asked to indicate in their papers *why* they are using the sources they have selected (rather than others) or to show *how* the quotations they use relate to their own ideas.

Students generally misuse sources out of a combination of ignorance of accepted procedures and a profound sense that they have no authority to say anything on their own. The solution to such misuse comes from a combination of clear discipline for breaking clearly stated rules and an educational program to help students gain a sense of intellectual identity. It is the essence of a college-level writing program to insist on active learning, to develop the individuality of the learner, and to help the learner differentiate other people's facts, ideas, and words from the learner's own words and experiences. The denial of the integrity of the self, which plagiarism expresses, should be seen in opposition to the whole idea of education.

Definition of Exit-Level Writing Skills

American liberal arts universities are not designed to impart specific quantities of knowledge. Even very complex licensure examinations, such as the medical profession's board exams or the legal profession's bar exams, seem inappropriate as models for measuring goals when we consider the wide-ranging function of the liberal arts degree: to "liberate" the mind and thereby create the free man and woman. Since college writing programs are the very essence of that liberal education, we must be careful in specifying what we mean by the writing ability required of college graduates. At the very least, we need to be aware that different kinds of institutions are likely to define that ability in different ways. We need also to be suspicious of oversimplified tests or other measures of that writing ability.

Nonetheless, we do have expectations that students receiving college degrees will be able to read and write better than they did upon entrance. Campuses with well-developed writing programs will have upper-division writing requirements that in practice enforce these expectations. Campuses without such programs may produce graduates who write so badly that they disgrace the institution. Most colleges in fact provide an unintended program for those who cannot or will not write; the courses that require only multiple-choice tests allow a path to the degree that weak or passive students readily discover. Such degree programs deny in practice the institution's goals; every campus has some kind of working consensus about how its graduates should be able to write.

A statement embodying those expectations is a useful guide to the institution, as well as to the students graduating from it. If the statement is sufficiently sophisticated, including an awareness of writing as a discovery and thinking process, it can lead to an upper-division writing program, if one does not already exist, or it can provide the criteria for a writing certification program, if one is called for. Such a statement can support writing-across-the-curriculum programs and other support programs within the various disciplines. Above all, it can assert unequivocally that the process of writing is a student's chief means of learning, just as an accomplished writing product is the sign of an educated individual. The only way a student can meet this kind of writing requirement is to accomplish the kind of reading, thinking, and writing that leaves one changed. And that is what our colleges and universities are for.

Chapter 8

Supporting, Evaluating, and Rewarding Writing Program Faculty

In June 1986, about two hundred participants at the Wyoming Conference on English passed a resolution speaking to what the *Association of Departments of English Bulletin* called "the increasing exploitation of English faculty members, particularly writing teachers" (Fall 1987, p. 50). That resolution was much debated in the profession (see *College English*, March 1987) and approved by both the Conference on College Composition and Communication (March 21, 1987) and the ADE Executive Committee (March 24, 1987). Since the resolution anticipates not only some kind of accreditation apparatus for composition programs but also letters of censure for institutions out of compliance, it is worth reprinting in full:

> WHEREAS, the salaries and working conditions of postsecondary teachers with primary responsibility for the teaching of writing are fundamentally unfair as judged by any reasonable professional standards (e.g., unfair in excessive teaching loads, unreasonably large class sizes, salary inequities, lack of benefits and professional status, and barriers to professional advancement);
>
> AND WHEREAS, as a consequence of these unreasonable working conditions, highly dedicated

teachers are often frustrated in their desire to provide students the time and attention which students both deserve and need;

THEREFORE, BE IT RESOLVED that the Executive Committee of [the Conference on] College Composition and Communication be charged with the following:

1. To formulate, after appropriate consultations with postsecondary teachers of writing, professional standards and expectations for salary levels and working conditions of postsecondary teachers of writing.

2. To establish a procedure for acting upon a finding of noncompliance; specifically, to issue a letter of censure to an individual institution's administration, board of regents or trustees, state legislators (where pertinent), and to publicize the finding to the public at large, the educational community in general, and to our membership.

We have, of course, seen this sort of thing before, and there is a good chance that nothing much will come of the proposed action. Even if the action is taken, there is a good chance that institutions will treat it as special pleading and pay no attention; several dozen institutions, after all, ignore the powerful black mark of censure by the American Association of University Professors for egregious violations of academic freedom. Besides, the CCC is not eager to take on the task that the resolution anticipates. At the 1988 CCC meeting, James C. Raymond, chair of the committee on implementing the Wyoming resolution, was quoted as saying that the CCC was not ready to deal with possible litigation and so would seek to work through existing organizations such as the Association of American University Professors and regional accrediting bodies (see Heller, 1988). Even if the Wyoming resolution is regarded as merely a sign of impotence and despair, colleges and universities certainly ought to examine their own policies to see whether they are contributors to the despair.

Institutions also should note that the approaching short-age of well-trained faculty in all fields, along with an already unmet demand for professional writing faculty, will give—indeed, already gives—new Ph.D.s in writing and rhetoric a wide choice of possible positions. Whether or not an accreditation or censure system is established, the campus with an advantage in professional working conditions for writing teachers will clearly be in a position to obtain the best faculty.

But many college administrators are unwilling to hear about the effects of institutional policies on writing teachers. When the writing classes are taught largely by part-time faculty, who sometimes must piece together such jobs at a number of institutions in order to survive on the fringes of the profession, the administration often closes its ears to tales of what such teachers go through: the "roads scholar" or "freeway flier" (as we call such faculty in California) dashes from campus to campus, sometimes driving hours a day between university, community college, and private college. Office hours to confer with students are impossible, with neither time nor office space available; no sense of institutional loyalty or collegiality can occur for teachers constantly on the move. It is obvious that the students of such faculty are being short-changed, however informed or dedicated the teacher may be. The institution is also losing much by this practice, despite the short-term financial benefit of hiring composition teachers by the course, at low piecework wages without fringe benefits. The advisory, departmental, and committee work that all faculty should do cannot be expected of these part-timers, nor can they contribute their ideas and energies to the development of the institution; the full-time faculty are usually asked to expand their university service to cover for the part-timers and to take a freeway flier to lunch now and again to foster collegiality.

Such abuses as the freeway flier are not unusual. As the Wyoming resolution makes clear, composition instruction in most American universities rests largely on the shoulders of part-timers and teaching assistants (TAs), who are keenly aware of their lack of status and power (and reward) within their institutions. I remember, for example, spending several days at a rural university with a generally good reputation; it was the only postsecondary institution in its area and, with its sound Ph.D. program, was known (accurately, as it turned out) for its scholarship as well as for its warm collegiality among the tenured faculty. I did note, when I reviewed the documents I had been sent in advance, that almost all of the composition teaching was done by TAs, but previous (in-house) evaluations of the freshman writing program spoke of training sessions for new TAs, seminars in the teaching of writing, and other support for the teachers. A different story—unhappily, a perfectly typical one—emerged as I heard from everyone involved.

At this university, English graduate students are required to teach one or two courses of freshman composition a term as part of their graduate work; a small salary is paid for the work, noticeably smaller (I learned late in my visit) for composition work than for any other teaching assistantship in the university. Many of the freshman sections are in fact taught by first-year graduate students, who arrive on campus in September with a literature bachelor's degree, the usual interest in advanced study of literature, and the usual need for enough money to survive; virtually none of the new graduate students had had any college training in the teaching of writing, and most of them had been exempted from their own freshman composition class, so their last experience with composition instruction was in high school English. These young people were given a two-day training session and introduction to the university by a harried WPA and then were given complete control over two classes of freshmen. I found no tenured or tenure-track faculty teaching freshmen at this university, and the seminar that supposedly helped the untrained instructors with their teaching had never met. (That mythical seminar had become a way for the university to grant a few graduate units to these teachers in lieu of adequate pay for their teaching.)

The closer I looked, the worse things appeared. The only organization or supervision for the freshman writing program took place among the graduate students themselves, informally. Even such important institutional committees as those developing a new curriculum for a second composition class were made up entirely of these graduate students, who, of course, were not paid to do committee work. Most of the administrators at the university felt that the situation was pretty successful: at little cost to the university, freshman composition was staffed, new graduate students picked up some money and on-the-job training, and no one important complained. The composition director gave me my first hint that all was not quite as splendid as the deans thought; she asked me to look closely at the situation, without quite saying why, and scheduled a session with the TAs with no regular faculty present.

That session was extraordinarily moving to me and remains vivid in my mind; it gives a kind of flesh and bones to the Wyoming statement (which, of course, was not restricted only to the situation of TAs). After repeatedly protesting their loyalty to the institution—which was, they noted with fairness and even gratitude, providing them subsistence wages to attend graduate school and gain graduate degrees—the TAs began to voice some bitter complaints. It was, they said carefully, very difficult to attend to their own studies, since the demands on their time were quite extraordinary, far beyond those made on the tenured faculty; for these TAs were full-time students as well as close to full-time teachers. These time demands, along with penury, were placing great pressure on young families and private lives. The professional pressures alone were immense. How is it possible to choose wisely between cheating one's students, who deserve more time than one has, and cheating oneself of library and study time? There was no useful support whatever from the tenured faculty, who were seen by this underclass as wealthy and with time to spare (which was, of course, far from the truth, except in comparison with themselves). The graduate students had mixed feelings about this lack of support, since it included lack of evaluation (except for a glance at a brief student survey); they saw the absence of evaluation as a blessed relief, though I saw it as one more abdication of responsibility by the institution.

Most moving of all, these overstressed young professionals did not place the blame where it belonged, on the institution that was exploiting them and the freshmen they were teaching.

On the contrary, and typically, they blamed themselves. "When I said good-bye to my students last term," one young woman said, her voice breaking, "I wanted to go down on my knees to them and beg their pardon for the terrible job I had done." As she described the way she had taught, fiercely red-marking errors and using frequent grammar drill, everyone had to agree with her assessment of her teaching. But who was responsible for giving her and her colleagues such a failure-ridden and traumatic introduction to the advanced study and basic work of the profession? Who owed the apology to the students?

Certainly, any institution that is serious about improving the campus climate for writing, and hence improving the education of its students, will pay serious attention to the treatment of its writing faculty. Administrators cannot expect complaints to initiate such action, since there are good reasons for all those involved to stay quiet. The entering freshmen have no real basis of comparison by which to ask for a higher-quality program than they receive and will put up with almost anything; the graduate students and part-time faculty are glad to have a toehold in the institution and are afraid to be known as troublemakers, since they are so expendable. And the full-time faculty benefit from the labor of the temporary writing teachers and therefore have many reasons and rationalizations for turning a blind eye to the abuse. Meanwhile, it takes considerable courage for an administration to look closely at a situation that is likely to cost substantial sums of money to improve. Responsible administration of a university or college writing program is a test of the institution's integrity, a test few institutions can pass at the minimum competence level.

Thus, we turn to a consideration of ways to support and evaluate those who teach and coordinate the writing courses that form the basis of the liberal arts curriculum. We will look in turn at the three general categories of evaluation that are used by many universities, though different kinds of institutions apply them with different emphases: teaching, professional growth and activity, and university service. Each of these categories takes on special characteristics in relation to the teaching of writing. For each category, I will consider first what it means to support these teachers and then what kinds of evaluation of them are likely to be appropriate.

Supporting and Evaluating the Teaching of Writing

Those responsible for supporting and evaluating the teaching of college faculty need to understand the difference between the teaching of writing and the teaching of many other college courses. Essentially, the teaching of writing requires a different kind of relationship between student and faculty than most other courses do, and calls for a much more steady pressure on the teacher to respond sensitively to student work. As every faculty member knows, particularly faculty from outside English who have taught writing in all-university programs, teaching writing is a particularly demanding and time-consuming job. The demand is a direct result of an unavoidably close student-faculty relationship.

In the first place, as suggested in Chapter Four, good writing teaching shifts the center of authority from the teacher to the student. The teacher must enable the student to develop a voice in control of the subject that the student is writing about. While the teacher can never, and should never, seek to give away ultimate evaluative responsibility (a fair final grade is part of the teacher's job), the best writing teachers often appear to be doing relatively little teaching or grading by conventional definitions. They will be working very hard devising appropriate writing tasks, responding to student drafts, talking with students about their writing, helping them evaluate and revise their work, presenting and challenging ideas, grading presentation drafts of papers, and the like, but they may never give a lecture. Almost inevitably, these fine teachers get to know their students well (the freshman composition teacher is an early warning system for potential suicide risks, for example), and their students in turn have the opportunity to get to know a serious advanced student (or even, sometimes, a practicing intellectual), often for the first time in their lives. In a very real sense, the writing class embodies the ideal of student and teacher on opposite ends of a log, an ideal that has receded into the realm of myth for undergraduates in most American universities, except for freshman composition. It is finally this constant pressure of work, combined with constant personal contact, that distinguishes the labor of writing teachers.

Support for Teaching. An institution that seeks to support the teaching of writing will expend funds to keep the student-faculty ratio low enough in writing courses so that these activities can go on. Once classes get above twenty or so, small-group work becomes difficult, and class discussion starts to disappear. The larger the group, the more passive the learning becomes, and passive learning contradicts writing instruction. If there are too many students, individual conferences about papers diminish in quantity and frequency; the instructor's view of revision starts to change from an essential teaching device to a doubling of the work load. The same problem compounds when teachers have more than one or two composition courses. The writing teacher who brings home a hundred papers for weekend reading every Friday will sacrifice any private life or some student learning. Few sensible teachers will persist in assigning much writing under such conditions. Why should the writing instructor, who is rarely paid more than other faculty, and normally paid a great deal less, spend so much more time on the job than anyone else?

The most important thing the institution can do for the writing teacher is to provide a manageable student load. Computer and tutoring labs, placement tests, upper-division requirements, writing-across-the-curriculum programs, conference travel, publication support—all of these are valuable and helpful. But a class of no more than twenty students is worth the whole cornucopia of other support for the teacher. The science lab with fifteen stations is of course limited to fifteen students, a wise limit provided by the expense of equipment that allows for good science teaching. The writing classroom has similar limitations, but they are less visible and hence easier to ignore, to the detriment of the writing program.

The second most important action an institution can take to support the teaching of writing is to review and improve the working conditions of its part-time writing teachers. A committee of the CCC is proposing a set of guidelines in this area, including these three standards:

- Generally, part-time faculty members should make up no more than 10 percent of writing instructors. They should be hired as early as possible, and be involved in setting departmental policy.
- Part-time faculty members should be paid at least 75 percent of the per-course salary for beginning full-time faculty members with comparable duties and credentials.
- Departments with the need should consider setting up a cadre of permanent part-time faculty members, who receive fringe benefits, merit raises, and have access to research support and travel funds [Heller, 1988, p. A7].

Campuses differ so widely in their situations that even these broad and reasonable standards will be unworkable for some institutions. What seems simply exploitative at one institution will appear, and perhaps be, fair at another. But every college interested in improving its campus climate for writing will find ways to treat these important faculty as real faculty, to relieve the invisibility and voicelessness that now diminishes them, and to give them access to the kind of institutional support that the statement envisions.

Evaluation of Teaching. The intense student-faculty relationship in writing instruction has an effect on student evaluations of teaching effectiveness, an important aspect of faculty evaluation on many campuses. The research on student evaluations is complex and mixed, but in practice they have substantial, even decisive, power on many campuses, particularly for part-time faculty or teaching assistants. I have read many hundreds of such student evaluations in faculty personnel files in all disciplines, alongside evaluations by colleagues, department chairs, and deans. The student evaluations, if conscientiously administered, have a compelling power, particularly if a specific kind of written comment occurs repeatedly from different classes over an extended period of years. These student perceptions of teaching ability tend to be consistent and reliable. But I always look at such evaluations of writing teachers differently than I do those of other faculty. Even the very best writing teachers have difficulty obtaining very high student ratings, though very low evaluations are often signs of genuine trouble. Good writing teachers are in the business of asking students to rethink, revise, edit their work; they not only challenge students the way all good faculty must, but they also are constantly returning student work with comments asking for more than many students want to give. I have, in fact, become suspicious of excessively high student ratings of writing teachers; if students are *that* contented with what the teacher has told them about their own work, I begin to wonder whether the level of instruction and commentary is too low. It is a rare student who will appreciate as good teaching (at the time) a steady demand to think yet more deeply and to revise yet once again.

Writing teachers should never be evaluated only by student perceptions, however well developed the rating form may be. Nor is a class visit by a colleague sufficient, though it may give a picture of the classroom portion of the instruction. The writing teacher's most important and time-consuming duties are to devise and respond to writing assignments and to hold conferences with students. At the least, therefore, the composition director or other class visitor should review assignments and revision schedules, read through a set or two of papers that contain the teacher's written responses, and discuss with the instructor the degree to which the course design integrates current knowledge of composition teaching.

A useful and extensive bibliography on evaluation of writing teachers appears in the second edition of *The Evaluation of Composition Instruction* (Davis and others, 1987). Just as students know that evaluation symbolizes real importance ("Will it be on the test?"), an institution shows the way it values composition instruction by the seriousness and responsibility with which it evaluates those who teach it.

Supporting and Evaluating Professional Growth

Support for Professional Growth. Nothing so distinguishes the professional work of writing faculty from traditional English faculty as does their scholarship. This scholarship tends to be misunderstood and depreciated by the English department and other faculty in the humanities, and hence is generally unsupported by the institution. A good friend and a fine literary scholar with whom I regularly play tennis brought this sad fact home to me some years ago. "What are you writing about these days?" he asked, with genuine interest, between sets. So I sent him an article I had recently published, relating current literary theory to the teaching of writing (White, 1984) and waited (in vain) for him to say something about it. Finally, I asked him if he had had a chance to look at it. "Oh, *that,*" he said, genuinely puzzled. "That's composition stuff. I meant your *real* work."

In fact, the "real work" of composition specialists tends to look very different from the literary scholarship of the usual English department member. Many English departments view textbooks, for example, as mere money-making devices, not to be taken seriously. But for the field of composition, an innovative and sound textbook makes an important contribution to the field. A few of them have gained classic status; others have changed the way hundreds of thousands of students are taught. (Some composition specialists are now producing computer software with the same result.) Nothing could be more logical than for new ideas about the teaching of writing to emerge in this practical form, but the prejudice against textbooks is deeply ingrained, and some English faculty actually regard a textbook as a black mark against a colleague.

Textbooks pose yet another problem. Such books are often written collaboratively, a practice common among scholars in the natural and social sciences but frowned on in the humanities. English departments, in particular, tend to be sympathetic to and supportive of an individual literary scholar, poring over minor masterpieces, emerging from the book stacks with a new interpretation; the composition scholar, working as part of a team producing and revising a textbook (or conducting the kind of research described in Chapters Two and Three), seems involved in some other enterprise, not really entitled to limited departmental funds or a lighter teaching load. With collaborative writing suspect, the composition specialist is in a poor position to compete for institutional support for the production of textbooks, or even for many other kinds of research in the field.

But composition faculty face a greater problem still when traditional English department committees review projects proposed for supported research. Composition research looks suspiciously like social science research, or even, to speak the unspeakable, education research. Admittedly, some composition faculty will routinely collaborate with colleagues in education or psychology, in part so that their projects can get a fair hearing outside the English department; and almost all composition research has pedagogical and social implications—a practical and often political goal that many English faculty regard as contrary to "real research." But although composition research looks odd or inappropriate to traditional English faculty, it is not in essence different from research in any other field. It borrows methodology from many fields but produces articles, books, reviews, and the like, along with its texts and software. It has the usual variation in quality, from journal to journal, from publisher to publisher, from one researcher to another. Indeed, when seen in the general university context, composition research is consistent with the kind of work most disciplines conduct: it attempts to produce useful knowledge, often using inductive and empirical procedures.

In research, as in pedagogy and curriculum, the English department needs the composition program even more than the composition program needs its literary and intellectual base. But something has to be done to channel institutional support into writing without passing it through a literary filter. Some English departments may in time grant sufficient representation to the writing program on key committees, so that composition research can begin to receive departmental support. On other campuses, the institutional writing program will have to find ways to funnel support from campus-wide bodies directly to composition faculty. As suggested in Chapter Seven, a campus administrator needs to oversee the entire writing program and serve as direct support to the WPA and the writing faculty.

Evaluation of Professional Growth. Just as we need to stress the difference of composition teaching from much of the other teaching that goes on in universities, we need to stress here the similarity of composition scholarship to scholarship in other fields. For too long, writing teachers have not been expected to conduct productive research in their field—mainly because they have been so overloaded with teaching that they had no time for anything else and also because writing scholarship has been so low in quality that publication did not have the same value or meaning that it had in other fields. Both of these conditions were at the same time causes and results of the academic depreciation of writing as a discipline and the apprentice status of most of the teachers. But these conditions are beginning to change in many institutions and at many journals.

In the fields of rhetoric and composition, there is the same wide variety of journals now as in most established fields: journals for empirical research (for example, *Research in the Teaching of English*), for practical teacher-scholars (*College Composition and Communication* or *College English*), and for special kinds of courses (*Freshman English News* or the *Journal of Advanced Composition*). There are regional journals, such as the University of Southern California's *Writing Instructor*, and historically oriented ones, such as the *Rhetoric Review.* Monograph series are sponsored by the National Council of Teachers of English, Southern Illinois University Press, Ablex, Prentice-Hall, and Random House, to mention only a few. Opportunities for book publishing have expanded greatly. Federal and private foundation grants are available to the innovative and the industrious. National and regional conferences are widely accessible to composition faculty and provide important opportunities for the presentation of new ideas. Therefore, it is time for composition teachers, researchers, and creative thinkers to receive the same respect, and hence to be subject to the same demands (and opportunities), as any other faculty members at their institutions.

Writing as a field of study offers ample opportunities for

scholars to demonstrate their scholarship for evaluation by their peers and by university committees. Institutions that demand signs of professional activity and publication from their faculty for promotion and tenure should expect exactly that from their writing faculty. The composition staff at universities should no longer be required to demonstrate their professionalism by publishing in other fields; evaluation committees should not assume that the "real work" of writing teachers is publication in literary journals. The field of composition is now ready to stand alongside any other discipline in the opportunities it offers for scholarship, research, and publication.

But this advance in opportunities for scholarship, publications, grants, and the like, is not all simple gain. Stephen North (1987) warns that the sudden affluence of the field is concentrated in a relative handful of textbook writers, consultants, and grant winners and that most laborers in the field remain burdened by too many students and too little pay to become competitors for university high stakes. Even more ominously, he cites signs that the scholars in the field are likely to use their prestige as their literary colleagues have always done—that is, to escape from the classroom: Robert Connors (1983) distinguishes "composition studies" from "composition teaching," and Carl Bereiter and Marlene Scardamalia (1983) suggest that their work might free researchers "from the pressure to show that their work is leading toward improvements in the teaching of writing" (quoted in North, 1987, p. 383).

In some institutions, the university reward system will be so inimical to the professional growth of writing faculty that they should not accept the system uncritically. It is all very well to say, as I do here, that composition specialists should be asked to contribute scholarship to their field; but if they continue to have a teaching load and working conditions that prohibit such scholarship, we are adding new cruelties, not professional possibilities. If the real function of scholarship at the institution is to allow the most creative faculty to escape teaching, rather than enrich it, then an evaluation system relying on scholarship will create a new subclass of the unpublished among writing faculty, the actual teachers of writing, with even lower status than before.

Here, as everywhere in the writing program, a single quick fix is likely to make matters worse rather than better. To simply impose scholarship requirements on the current writing faculty in most postsecondary institutions, without reviewing and improving their lot, would be morally wrong and personally destructive. The professionalization of writing faculty must be seen as part of the overall improvement of the campus climate for writing, a result of the improvement much more than its cause.

Supporting and Evaluating University Service by Writing Teachers

Support for University Service. All good teachers talk with their students. But the composition class calls for unremitting communication between student and teacher week after week. For this reason, the composition instructor often serves as a general adviser for the students in his or her classes. "You are the only one I can talk to around here, the only one who seems really interested in me," the student will say halfway into the term, settling into the seat beside the desk. The teacher hears this familiar sentence with a combination of warmth and dread: warmth because teaching is a helping profession and human contact is one of its principal rewards; dread because that opening gambit leads into harrowing, painful, risky conversations. The sensitive teacher will know when this kind of counseling moves into areas where trained personnel should be called in; writing teachers are not psychological counselors or social workers. But sometimes students' lives are changed as a result of an intense conversation with a concerned mentor.

The best institutions will support and foster this kind of faculty-student contact. (The Oxford-Cambridge tutorial system probably is the prime example.) The crucial moment in my own education occurred when my freshman composition teacher Hans Gottlieb asked me, in his office at New York University, why I wanted to be a businessman. "Because I want to make a lot of money," I replied, giving the only answer my family and my culture had provided me with at the age of eighteen. "That's not a good enough reason," he said, stunning me into a thoughtful silence. The conversation that followed changed my life, and I am by no means unique. But I wonder whether that same conversation could have taken place, or could have had the same result, if my teacher had been the usual harried TA, showing signs of frantic poverty, talking to me in the corridor because no office space could be spared.

Evaluation of University Service. To do the job effectively, the writing teacher must spend time with students beyond the requirements of ordinary office hours and beyond the reasonable limits for most other faculty. Institutions evaluating writing faculty need to find ways not only to support and encourage conference and advisement time but to evaluate (perhaps through student evaluations) and reward productive teachers for what they do outside as well as inside the classroom.

Finally, I must return to the college service performed by the writing program administrator, the true hero of this book, and an appropriate protagonist for the end of this chapter. I have elsewhere in this book referred to the overwhelming numbers of tasks that WPAs find themselves attempting to accomplish. I have been both a department chair and a WPA, and there is no question in my mind that the WPA has a far more demanding job in every way—with far less support, prestige, and assigned time for the task. Aspects of the job range around the entire university, including various kinds of responsibilities for tests, faculty appointments, faculty development and evaluation, student grade appeals, curriculum development, budgets, even advice on usage and grammar to the university president preparing a speech. The job is complex, time consuming, and emotionally draining. It combines sharply limited authority with high levels of responsibility. It is not, as some evaluation committees seem to believe, just another committee assignment. Therefore, evaluation committees need to be aware that a candidate who has performed this demanding job successfully has rendered a valuable service to the institution.

It should, perhaps, come as no surprise that the WPA as administrator receives little recognition or evaluation. American colleges and universities, consumed though they are with constant evaluations of faculty, generally conduct rather perfunctory reviews of their administrators. The contrast is often striking: documents for evaluation of faculty go on for many pages, describing permissible publications and distinguishing between "adequate" and "competent" teaching; evaluations of deans might consist of a casual poll of faculty, asking whether the administrator seems all right. Whereas a series of elected committees evaluate faculty, in part to ensure that they meet stated criteria and that personal relationships cannot form the basis of judgment, many administrators are evaluated according to how well they get along with the next administrator up the line. It does not seem exorbitant to ask that administrative jobs, as well as faculty or staff positions, be evaluated according to stated criteria or that clear performance evaluations seek to discover how well these criteria have been met. If such reasonable and consistent evaluation practices were in effect, the scope of the WPA's job would be apparent from the criteria for evaluation, and the WPA's value would be more obvious to those assessing his or her performance.

Under present circumstances, the most efficient way for the evaluation committees to understand the significance of the WPA's work is for the English department chair to make a particular point of what it means. At present, with so many English departments split in their attitudes toward the writing programs they house, the chair may or may not make this case. But whether or not the English department is comfortable with the wide-ranging effect and importance of the writing program, the work of the WPA deserves support and recognition. In some universities, only a central administrator—perhaps the administrator I argued for in Chapter Seven—can fully evaluate and demonstrate the importance of the WPA. No action taken by the administration so fully expresses the campus climate for writing as its recognition of the campus writing program administrator.

The dilemma for writing teachers, and those who support and evaluate them, is in some ways more severe than it is for other university teachers. Composition faculty normally have a higher and more demanding work load, and their status and pay are lower. Yet the university asks for more than teaching of all its faculty; writing teachers must also write and publish if composition as a field of study is to continue to gain the recognition within the academic community that it deserves. If we are to argue that a larger number of regular faculty should join the TAs and part-timers in the composition classrooms, and that the exploitation of the TAs and part-timers must stop, we must be able to point to the scholarship as well as to the teaching task that allows the writing faculty to claim a lower work load. And then we must see to it that working conditions will improve to the point that the writers will choose to stay in the writing classroom even if they do not have to. Finally, we must recognize that the job of the writing teacher extends beyond the classroom, just as we expect education itself to do. No simple solution will improve this circular problem, but a college that considers writing at the center of its education will recognize the special needs for support and evaluation of its writing faculty.

Chapter 9

Preparing and Certifying Writing Instructors for Colleges and Schools

The recent advances in knowledge about the teaching of writing seem to have left college and university training programs for prospective teachers almost entirely untouched. In-service programs, for teachers already in the schools, have been more responsive. A major in-service effort of multinational proportions, which began as the (San Francisco) Bay Area Writing Project, has for the last decade been conducting university summer workshops (with much additional local training conducted by those trained in the workshops) for selected working teachers. This "National Writing Project," under the direction of James Gray, at the University of California, Berkeley, consisted of 166 separate local writing project sites as of December 1987. Many thousands of teachers have participated in these workshops across the country and elsewhere and have been at least exposed to such concepts as the importance of the writing process, the uses of peer reading and holistic evaluating of student work, the ineffectiveness of formal grammar instruction for improving writing, the definition of writing as a part of thinking and learning, and other matters discussed elsewhere in this book. However, the *preservice* education programs through which these teachers pass on their way to certification remain very much as they were, with very little attention given to writing or writing instruction.

Because the various disciplines in the university are relatively isolated from one another, and because writing research has had little impact even on the composition programs of many English departments, many education departments are unaware that changes are now needed in the training of writing teachers. Traditionally, education departments have left subject matter to the other departments; writing has appeared to be a subject matter to the education faculty, while it has appeared pedagogical to those in English. Hence, the matters dealt with in this book have fallen between two schools and have almost never been part of teacher training, an odd paradox indeed.

Because of this failure on the part of the universities, the teachers recruited for the National Writing Project's in-service workshops, who are normally the most professional and intellectually vigorous ones in their districts, frequently speak of their teacher training programs with disrespect. When writing was dealt with at all (which is itself unusual), it seemed to appear as handwriting, mechanics, grammar, or (worst of all) discipline: "If you don't behave, you will have to write!" An occasional teacher of a methods course might have mentioned the writing process, or the course in reading may have cast a brief glance at writing as a part of reading instruction, but in general the education programs find no time for much focus on writing and its central role for learning. English departments have been content to leave such instruction to the education departments, while the rest of the university has left it to the English department.

Since grade school teachers spend roughly half of their instructional time teaching writing and reading, and since many high school teachers would profit from the use of writing in their classrooms, it is clearly time for the preservice teacher training programs to introduce courses in the teaching of writing. To be sure, the curriculum is already crowded and under pressure, as are the schools of education themselves. They are being asked to improve the education of teachers, and to stiffen credential requirements for teachers, with very little support from the society as a whole or from the rest of the university. Nonetheless, many education programs have earned their reputation for low standards, weak students, and minimal requirements.

It is for this reason that some states, such as California and Virginia, have abolished the education major as an undergraduate program; several recent reports have urged all states to do so as a principal means of upgrading teacher preparation. When education becomes a graduate program, the argument goes, students will need to have an academic major before admission and hence will have some area of specialization to build on as teachers. Concentrated study in one field will enable these prospective teachers to develop their thinking, analytical power, and knowledge in some depth. A highly professional graduate program can then build on this foundation, leading to certification and the master's degree.

While such a plan has great potential, particularly for high school teachers, it by no means necessarily leads to major changes in the quality of teacher preparation programs or their faculties. Nor will the plan by itself change the abilities of the students entering the field. The quality of students in education programs is determined more by the status and pay they can look forward to in the teaching profession than by the level and name of the training program. And when an education program is defined as a graduate program, students are even less likely to learn about the teaching of writing. Not unreasonably, the education department will assume that the college graduates it admits have already achieved writing competence. In California, where there has been no undergraduate education major for many years, instruction in the teaching of writing still remains a hit-or-miss affair, usually missed.

Besides, the usual academic major leaves out much that is useful for grade school teachers, who are called on to teach every subject to a single class. Because these teachers need to know something about almost everything, general majors (called "liberal studies" or the like) quickly emerge to replace the academic major. These general majors, which require a bit of study in many fields, eventually begin to resemble the old education majors, as their academic content gets thinner under the pressure of all the things teachers should know: not only reading, writing, and arithmetic but also such subjects as nutrition, drug education, sex and health education, and child development. It becomes hard to think of an expanded general education program, with some education emphasis, as an "academic major," with its demand for some depth of knowledge. Once again, as with the old education major, the weakest students gravitate to this relatively undemanding course of study. Meanwhile, education departments understandably seek to offer more and more undergraduate credits in these majors for school teachers. Teaching internships, for example, logically insert themselves into such majors on the reasonable grounds that students should see for themselves whether they are suited for the classroom. These liberal studies programs can offer prospective teachers a good background at the beginning level in a number of fields, but no one should imagine that they offer a high-quality curriculum to more able students.

California's attempt to improve teacher preparation by removing the old undergraduate education major has, I think, improved the preparation of high school teachers, who now must have a college major in the academic field they teach. But the crucial elementary grades have not been much touched by the change. Nor does the legislation ensure that more able students will enter teaching or that they will be informed about such ideas as the importance of writing for thinking. The problems of increasing teacher quality in general and of developing teacher training in the pedagogy or practice of writing in particular are far more complex and resistant to easy answers than they seem to be.

Certification Tests as a Means of Increasing Teacher Quality

When we begin to speak of professional qualifications for teachers, in relation to assessment programs, we immediately run into the basic contradiction in American society in relation to schools and those who teach the children in them. We say we want highly qualified teachers, but we are unwilling to grant teachers the pay, the working conditions, or the status that would draw highly qualified individuals into the teaching profession. For various reasons, this contradiction has become politically and economically uncomfortable in recent years, and several proposed solutions to it have appeared. One of the least expensive, and hence most attractive, is to imagine that we can solve this dilemma by way of assessment. In some ways, assessment is an ironically inappropriate solution, since most of the assessment devices that are proposed actually embody this contradiction by simultaneously *raising* standards, by way of standardized tests and other requirements, and *lowering* standards, by requiring the schools to find ways around those requirements for those wishing to teach but unable to meet them; the schools, after all, must staff classrooms with the many teachers they need and will need as the teacher shortage gets worse, even if the job is not attractive enough to enlist those we would assess as fully qualified.

The contradiction thus remains inescapable. As the standards for teachers get higher, fewer and fewer students will be able to meet them. For example, according to a new policy in the California State University, only those students with grade point averages in the top half of their academic major will be admitted into the (graduate) teaching programs. Everyone has applauded this bold move for teacher quality. For far too long, we have been recruiting our teachers from the bottom half of the student body; now they will come from the top half. But when we say this, we fail to recognize that we have not been *prohibiting* students from the top half of the class from entering teaching or staying in teaching; nor do we contemplate *compelling* or even seriously *inducing* those students into teaching. We are screening out the weaker students but are not providing incentives for the stronger ones to become teachers instead of doctors, lawyers, bankers, computer scientists, research chemists, or business executives.

The wide career opportunities now available for women of this generation have increased the problem of recruiting teachers; many of the women now in the law, medical, and business schools would, even a generation ago, have been in teacher training programs. We have mostly lost that captive population of competent women for teaching, and we are in the process of turning away the less competent (or at least the nonstandardized) students through our assessment devices; but who is to take their place?

We must put the assessment of teachers into this larger

social context if it is to make sense or to have any effect. Those who imagine that teacher certification tests can by themselves improve the quality of teachers, while salaries and working conditions remain relatively unchanged, are deceiving themselves and their constituencies. If the tests screen out too many prospective teachers, school districts will have to hire uncertified teachers under what some states call "emergency credentials." The teacher shortages now predicted in most states suggest that strenuous efforts will be needed if teacher quality is not to sink even below what it is now. Many plans are afloat, as we keep hearing from the well intentioned and the politically active, to improve teacher salaries, career ladders, conditions, and the like. Until some real funding appears to implement these good intentions, our best students will continue to resist the undoubted appeal of teaching as a career for those who want meaningful, humane work.

But assessment does have an important role to play. As we read through the statements by those critical of the present state of the schools, it seems clear that a demonstrable improvement in the quality of teachers—demonstrated by assessment—is one key to improvements in salary and working conditions. Just as we protect tenure by firing those who abuse their tenured status, we confirm arguments for the improvement of teaching conditions by overtly screening out the unqualified. Perhaps in time we can ask more from our assessments, perhaps even use them to identify the best as well as the worst; our concern for the near future must be to meet the pressing need for teachers while protecting standards as well as we can. If we are particularly wise, we can also use this urge toward assessment to come up with better assessment devices than we now use.

A recent compilation of information by the Educational Commission of the States (Bray and others, 1985) provides impressive news about the increase in the quantity of teacher certification tests. Two years before that report, in 1983, twenty states were testing the competence of candidates for teaching certificates, and numbers of other states were considering the possibility (Flakus-Mosqueda, 1983, p. vi). Just two years later, the number of states mandating such testing had moved up to thirty-four. By the fall of 1987, according to an official of the American Association for Higher Education, all fifty states had mandated such tests (Marchese, 1987). Furthermore, many institutions are starting to use tests such as the California Basic Educational Skills Test (CBEST) and the Educational Testing Service's National Teachers Examination (NTE) to screen applicants for entry into teacher training programs, as well as for certification of skills after program completion. After all, students who do not pass the screening test should be informed about their shortcomings before they embark on a teacher training program (particularly if they are college graduates); they also should be told that they will not receive certification if they are unable to pass a similar test after they complete the "professional" education program.

While all this activity is going on, there has been relatively little discussion about the criteria for the certification devices that have blossomed around the country. Tests often are chosen, or even written, without much attention to the criteria that are appropriate for the particular situation. It is, of course, far easier to give a handy existing test with an appropriate-sounding name than to ask the necessary troubling questions: What are the writing and reading skills we should require of those we will license to teach our young? And what kind of assessment program is most likely to test these skills reasonably and fairly?

An assessment of writing ability for teachers should not only require real writing, as the CBEST and the NTE now do, but also should assess a candidate's ability to teach writing. Therefore, prospective teachers should be asked to create or at least recognize effective writing topics, to come up with prewriting activities, to respond sensitively and usefully to first drafts, and to help students revise their work. Most of all, the teacher candidate should show an ability to produce and respect writing as real communication and a real means to discovery and learning. In addition, prospective teachers must be able to respond in an unbiased manner to the writing of racial and cultural minorities. Although teachers cannot and should not be free of their own cultural contexts, they should be able to recognize and cope with different cultures and dialects without automatically calling them wrong. No test that I know of even begins to examine such matters.

Reading tests for teachers are, if anything, in even worse shape than writing tests are. Almost all reading tests assume that the text given on the examination actually contains one clear meaning and that the good reader will discover this correct meaning; the good reader will then presumably come up with the "right answer" to a multiple-choice question designed to elicit that one answer. As with error recognition items, the reading tests work this way largely because a belief in single right answers dominates much educational ideology, reflecting the simple-minded political, religious, and moral views that have become prominent in recent years; not coincidentally, this view also leads to cheap testing and consistent statistics. But I can't imagine anything more destructive to the teaching of reading than the hunt for unambiguously right answers. Reading, as the wise current slogan puts it, is a psychological guessing game, an adventure, a joint effort by reader and writer to *create* (not just passively discover) meaning. Contemporary reading theory disputes (sometimes with considerable dogmatism of its own) the assumption that meaning is only a property of the text. But if we are to include in our reading tests contemporary concerns with the process of reading and the ways in which readers make meaning, we need to abandon the multiple-choice format and the assumptions about single right answers that they embody—an expensive prospect that test makers have yet to undertake. I know of no readily available reading test that has gained the respect of the most informed reading specialists.

Recent developments in the testing of writing offer important opportunities for improvement in the testing of reading. Certainly, essay testing allows a student to describe the meanings obtained by the reading process that led to those meanings. But the traditional assumption that reading and writing are different skills, requiring different kinds of measures, stands in the way of such a development. That assumption is open to question, however, and flies in the face of much teacher experience. We need new examinations that find ways of combining the reading test with the writing test—they are both exercises in the understanding and making of meaning—and reward those who have some feeling and passion for words, ideas, and creativity. As things go today, many of our teachers, even English teachers, do not read for pleasure and hate to write. How can they help but convey these same attitudes to their students?

Some of these problems can begin to yield to practical solutions when an institution is determined to take the certification of teachers seriously. At the California State University, for example, every candidate for entry into a teacher training program must now be examined by the faculty of the student's major and subsequently recommended by that faculty. It has been a taxing but not impossible task for one of the largest teacher training institutions (through the master's degree) in the world. In addition to the departmental test, which contains both written and oral components, most students must also pass the CBEST upon entry into teacher training. The school of education then assesses other matters, such as the candidate's ability to deal with children and to manage classroom chaos. Many cynical faculty, including me, have been astounded to see how readily and how seriously our departmental colleagues have undertaken the immense task of participating in teacher certification. They have done so, I am convinced, because they themselves—and not a school of education or an outside testing organization—have been made responsible for establishing criteria and procedures and for developing and scoring the assessments. I recommend this certification process as an important advance in screening of prospective teachers, but I have no illusions that it will improve teacher quality unless or until a larger number of the best students can be induced to enter teacher training programs.

I have been focusing here on assessments designed for teachers. But we should not overlook the problems posed for these teachers by the tests designed for their students, since the teacher tests in some sense must echo them. When I talk with the best school teachers, I am invariably told that the major obstacle they face in the teaching of writing is the proficiency test that is used to determine the effectiveness of their teaching and their school's success. When that test turns out to be a multiple-choice usage or mechanics test—as it usually does—the teacher must decide whether to teach to the test or to teach writing. A very few will focus on the discovery and creativity that real writing offers to their students, knowing that their students are likely to do just as well on the test as those buried in workbooks. But even the students will know that ignoring direct test preparation is risky business in a test-oriented world. The assessment states what matters for real, and in most cases it is not writing.

Where Can Prospective Teachers Learn About the Teaching of Writing?

If we accept the premise that a sound preservice teacher training program will include serious and informed instruction in writing and the teaching of writing, and if we notice that almost none of that is now included in these programs, we are forced to face a practical dilemma. At present, neither the education department nor the English department is likely to assume responsibility for requiring or even teaching this material unless some administrative initiative urges them to do so. As long as each department regards such teaching as the other's job—and surely no other department is able to do the task—teachers will lack the training they need and deserve to have. These departments have disclaimed responsibility largely because their faculties were unable to teach writing to teachers and were not interested in the teaching of writing as a genuine career in itself.

As we move toward and into the 1990s, that situation is likely to change. According to a Modern Language Association survey of doctoral programs in English conducted in 1986, "34 percent report having programs in rhetoric, writing, and composition, and another 6 percent plan to establish one. Half of the rhetoric programs were established three to eight years ago" (Huber, 1988, p. iii). Robert D. Denham, editor of the *Association of Departments of English Bulletin,* believes that these figures reflect "the most striking change in the graduate curriculum that has occurred during the past fifteen years" (1987, p. ii). Let us assume, optimistically, that these figures and Denham's response turn out to reflect reality, as they may. With doctoral programs increasingly producing trained specialists in writing, and with many English departments beginning (if grudgingly) to recognize writing as a respectable field of specialization, we can look forward to a near future in which most institutions will be able to staff the needed courses for teachers. Indeed, these new faculty are likely to be devising and promoting such courses on many campuses, since they are trained to be keenly aware of the need.

The English department, as I said earlier, is the natural home for writing courses, and the American university experience has demonstrated that belief by its practice. Even when the English department has sought to avoid responsibility for writing instruction and has undervalued both students and faculty in the program (as some still do), most universities have persisted in allotting the composition program to English. As I have argued in earlier chapters, those who specialize in language and literature have a natural affinity for the written word (even if it is written by students). As English departments begin to accept this responsibility (indeed, if the MLA survey is to be believed, to welcome it), they should begin to offer the necessary courses for prospective teachers.

In short, I think that every prospective teacher should be required to take a course in the teaching of writing offered by a writing specialist in the English department. In order to pass the course, the student should be required not only to understand and apply what is known about the teaching of writing but also to write at an adequate level. The curriculum for such a course offers a new kind of challenge to the new kind of English faculty who will be teaching it. Such a course would foster and validate the kind of assessment device I have been proposing.

As the National Writing Project has demonstrated, writing itself must be at the heart of this required course. At the same time, prospective teachers should be introduced to the substantial body of available information on writing and writing instruction. But the course cannot merely ask students to repeat information about writing. It must also require that the students in the class write constantly, in many modes of expression, as a way of learning the material they study.

The prospective teachers in this class should thus be assigned journals, letters, poetry, stories, and personal essays as well as the usual expository writing. James Britton and his colleagues (1975) have shown that, in the London schools, the range of writing assignments is very narrow and (they imply) very boring. Arthur Applebee (1981) has shown that American classrooms also are not exactly lively. Although the course I am describing cannot turn boring teachers into exciting ones, it can expand the writing experiences of those enrolled. Only teachers who have themselves written stories or journals or the like can share with their students the excitement and discovery that these writings offer. Most teachers avoid poetry in their classrooms because they fear it, from lack of awareness and experience; yet even deprived youngsters are able to write poetry with real excitement when given the chance (see Koch, 1970).

This class also should involve its students in responding to each other's work. Teachers need to learn how to help each other appropriately at various stages in the writing process and how to help other writers develop a sense of audience. They also need to read about effective ways of responding to writing and to practice these responses in the class, in groups as well as individually. At the same time, the course needs to attend to the creation of appropriate writing assignments, probably the most neglected aspect of every teacher's preparation (see Chapter Four). And every high school teacher should understand and know how to teach the responsible use of sources.

Finally, the English department should not be content with offering a single course in the teaching of writing; English needs to become much more involved in the preservice curriculum planning that is now wholly (or largely) in the domain of the education department. The English department's required course—with its emphasis on writing—should be supported by writing requirements in other teacher preparation courses; courses in cognitive growth should include material on the role of writing in cognition; and writing and reading should be given the importance in the teacher training curriculum that they have in the schools. It is wholly appropriate for English departments (as some now do) to offer their own "methods" courses for prospective teachers, if the department has hired qualified faculty to do so, and to supervise student teachers in the field. If the field of composition and the teaching of writing develop over the next decade along the lines of the past decade, such an extension of English departments into the traditional turf of the education department is bound to occur. Whether this change is welcomed by the education department or resisted by it, as academic tradition suggests, it must occur if the teaching of writing is to improve in the nation's schools.

School-College Collaboration in Writing Instruction

While the most significant action that postsecondary institutions can take to help the schools teach writing more effectively is to improve teacher training, much more can and ought to be done. School-college in-service workshops, as the National Writing Project has shown, can have substantial impact. But such workshops are only a beginning. A recent volume gives sixteen examples of constructive collaboration between schools and colleges, most of them involving writing instruction (Fortune, 1986). Joint projects to improve the writing of college-bound students appear a natural extension of collegiate concern over preparation for freshman composition and of school concern for the success of graduates. However, any college administrator setting out to work with the schools, or any college writing teachers seeking to collaborate with high school English teachers, should be aware that the task is far more difficult than it appears to be. Even well-meaning attempts on the part of postsecondary institutions to work with the schools have historically worked badly, for reasons that are useful to explore. College faculties and administrations moving into this area ought to avoid the mistakes of the past.

The usual pattern of school-college relationships works this way: University faculty and administrators (with little or no consultation) develop an agenda, invite school teachers to attend a session to hear about what they are doing wrong and to be told how they should change, and are astonished to find that the visiting teachers are not only ungrateful for the information (and the wine and cheese) but positively antagonistic to the whole process. Instead of placidly taking notes and blame, the school teachers are likely to assert that the university folk have no understanding of what things are like in the schools and, in short, don't know what they're talking about. Some ways of breaking this destructive pattern are described in "Who Do You Think You're Talking To?: Trading Ideas for Insults in the English Profession" (McQuade, 1976).

The National Writing Project has been able to get beyond that pattern, largely by a continuing effort to value the work and knowledge of the school teachers selected to participate. This project also breaks the pattern by establishing new identities (as writers as well as teachers) for the participants (Schultz and others, 1988). Even a casual observer is bound to notice (often with considerable surprise) the prominent role of the school teachers in every aspect of the National Writing Project and the heightened sense of professionalism and community that they express. Not every campus will want to follow the National Writing Project model, but the reasons for its endurance and influence are well worth examining and duplicating.

The Schultz study of school-college interactions posits a profound cultural difference as the underlying reason for the failure of most attempts to collaborate: "School and college writing teachers are members of different cultures and . . . a number of factors within each culture can help explain why common action is difficult" (p. 145). One set of cultural differences emerges from the different working conditions: time, material goods, and rewards are more available on college campuses. (Neither "culture" has a reward system that much encourages participation, however.) More profound still are "three beliefs that may prevent high school and college writing teachers from collaborating successfully: (1) that schools and colleges should exist in a hierarchical relationship with each other; (2) that knowledge should be created at advanced levels of the educational system and applied or carried out at lower levels; and (3) that the language and discursive practices of each educational level should be separate and distinct" (pp. 146–147). Anyone contemplating a project to bring school and college writing teachers together should consult this study; while it refrains from suggesting what ought to be done, it gives a thoughtful and convincing map of what ought not to be done and why.

Despite these difficulties, many colleges and universities will find ways to bring school and college teachers together to explore ways to improve student writing. Different campuses will reach out to different groups of teachers; these teachers must have a substantial voice in determining the agendas that can be cooperatively pursued. Some teachers will need in-service training; others will need help with assessment; others, perhaps, will require master's degrees or help with English as a second language. Perhaps a teacher exchange program, with some kinds of classroom exchanges, would be a creative idea. Colleges need also to ask what they can learn, as well as what they can teach, in the process. Once the "cultural conflicts" are recognized and dealt with, all kinds of possibilities open up. The systems are inexorably linked by students, by the discipline, by funding. (A legislator asked me at a hearing into a public university request for remedial writing funds, "Why should the people have to pay for this twice?") The schools, with their overburdened and undertrained writing teachers, need regular help and support; the colleges, with their weak teacher training programs, also need help and support. Postsecondary education cannot merely stand aloof and complain, and then arrogantly seek to "remedy" what it has ignored and, to some degree, helped to bring about. If we expect students to arrive on our campuses already understanding that writing is a way of thinking and learning, we cannot simply train the teachers and ignore them after they leave campus. The teachers, however well trained, are indeed in a different culture from that of their professors, and they need the professional links, revitalization, and status that postsecondary institutions can provide. We cannot expect students to understand that writing is central to the liberal arts and to their education if that idea meets them for the first time in college. The school teachers must introduce them to this idea, early on and steadily. No one can undertake such a task without the substantial support postsecondary education needs to struggle to provide.

Chapter 10

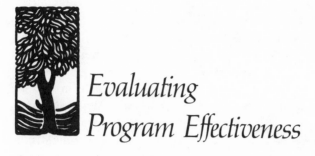

Evaluating
Program Effectiveness

"Everything should be as simple as possible—but no simpler."

—Albert Einstein

One of the strangest experiences in my academic life was testifying before the California Senate Committee on Finance. In the spring of 1978, I was the faculty consultant in English testing to the California State University (CSU) system, which had recently inaugurated a statewide English Placement Test. The program was incomplete, since (for odd historical reasons) our huge system still had no funded program for students who scored at the low range of that test. We were asking the legislature to appropriate some millions of dollars to inaugurate such a program, and I was the expert witness before the committee. Our task was made particularly difficult by the looming shadow of Proposition 13, the property tax limitation initiative, which everyone sensed was sure to be approved by the voters that fall, and which would cut severely the funding source for public education.

So there I sat at a scarred table in a Sacramento hearing room, craning my neck up at the senators sitting on their raised platform, with an experienced and rather distrustful dean-of-getting-money-from-the-legislature sitting by my elbow. I felt nervous—as if I were playing a strange game where I was unsure of the rules, though I had been carefully but (as it turned out) inadequately prepped. The chair of the Committee on Finance, a venerable but notoriously shrewd sheep rancher from the central valley, peered down at me and asked the question that everyone wants to know about any test. "Tell me, Professor," he said, not unkindly, "how many students flunked that test of yours this past fall?"

I was ready for the question and had prepared a careful response. "I can't give you a simple number, Senator," I said. "The test is designed to give a profile of student skills, not just a pass or fail. We report a set of six separate scores to each campus for each student; the campus then analyzes the scores and places the student appropriately in whatever curriculum the campus has in place for entering students." I sat back, feeling that I had started out just fine.

But the senator was frowning, and when he spoke he was no longer friendly. "Just like a professor!" he barked at no one in particular. "You ask a simple question and all you get back is a bunch of gobbledygook!"

The dean at my elbow sensed disaster and sprang into action. "Senator," he called out, "we estimate that fully half of those who took the test failed it."

The bottom dropped out of my stomach. Early on, all of us involved in the program had decided that a system-wide cutting score on the placement test made no sense, since we were dealing with nineteen campuses of widely varying purposes and quality. A student with writing ability that cried out for improvement on a small liberal arts campus might have quite acceptable literacy for an agriculture program at a polytech. We would not report scores as passing or failing apart from campus programs, and we would not report scores in a way that might lead to misuse of what we saw as a descriptive profile. While there were some opposing arguments, the agreement had been so clear that the issue had not come up again, not until this moment, when the dean proclaimed—really invented—decisions and data that simply did not exist. I held my breath.

The senator had turned from me and was now smiling at the dean. "Well now, Dean," he went on, "just how do you come by that number?"

How, indeed! But the dean never wavered. "You see, Senator," he said, smooth as vinyl, "that's about the number that scored below the fiftieth percentile." He smiled. The senator smiled. Everybody smiled. The dean had resolved the question by stating that the lower half of scores was the lower half of scores. It was rather like that comic scene in the film *Amadeus* where the emperor tells Mozart his music has "too many notes." What did the fact that there was a lower half of scores have to do with the determination of how many failed? But the dean knew his audience. "Thank you," said the now genial sheep rancher. "It's a relief to have *somebody* at that table who can give a straight answer when we need one."

And, soon after this nonsensical answer that appeared (to one of the shrewdest minds in the legislature) to be straightforward and simple, right under the clouds of the approaching Proposition 13 hurricane, the CSU received its millions of dollars to establish remedial programs for students scoring in the lower half on our English Placement Test. That funding continues today and has helped tens of thousands of ill-prepared students stay, and succeed, in college. It has also, as I indicated in Chapters Six and Seven, allowed the freshman writing program to improve and the upper-division writing program to develop. And none of this would have happened if the dean had not, shall we say, simplified the data.

I recount this story because, like the Bakersfield politician, most people who ask for program evaluations think that they are entitled to simple answers; and, also like our senator, they usually are happier with simple and false answers than with real responses—which, alas, are almost never simple. My motto for such matters comes from Albert Einstein, who also would have been a terrible flop before a senatorial committee: "Everything should be as simple as possible—but no simpler." For some interesting reasons, many otherwise intelligent and responsible people, even those who know that educational issues are complicated, feel that measurement problems must have easy answers.

Thus, I don't think that some politicians are aberrant when they misuse the College Board's Scholastic Aptitude Test as a scorecard for the public schools. Nor are all the admissions officers who ignore the standard error of measurement on college aptitude tests. Nor is the California education official who told me, after misreading some data, "Now that we have solved the reading problem, we can turn our attention to writing." Nor is the parent from Huntington Beach who shouted her frustration at teachers during a school board meeting on proficiency tests: "We're paying you to *educate* our kids; stop messing with their *minds.*" No one likes to be told that things are more complicated than they seem or ought to be. Everyone wants measurement to reduce the complexity of the world to manageable numbers and hence manageable concepts.

I don't want to commit the error I am warning against by oversimplifying the demand for program evaluation. Everything *should* be as simple as possible, and in general one function and purpose of evaluation is to simplify complex phenomena. We sample a universe and report a score. Program evaluation, after all, is designed to satisfy the demand that an instructional program (or a grant, or an in-service training project, or a research design) demonstrate that it has helped someone improve in a measurable way. What could be more reasonable? Why do we have to insist that it is all very complicated? Why can't we give a simple answer to the simple question? Since we recognize, as we must, the right to ask whether our programs are doing anybody any good, why do we stumble and stutter and talk gobbledygook in reply?

I looked briefly at a certain kind of program evaluation in Chapter Six, including it in the context of institutional testing programs. I suggested there that reducing program evaluation to pre/post testing or to "value-added" schemes is ineffective and inappropriate, although my experience with the sheep rancher keeps me aware that even shrewd observers want and need such simplifications. In this chapter, I want to focus on the issues, problems, and possibilities of program evaluation in some detail. The problem of program evaluation is particularly interesting not merely because such evaluations often influence a program's funding, or even its existence, but because they focus and distill the essence of the problems we have with testing and with teaching writing in general.

Nonempirical Evaluations

Nonempirical methods of program evaluation have some value and some place, but they are, by themselves, inadequate to the task. They represent attempts to solve the difficult problems of writing program evaluation with solutions that turn out to be too simple.

Evaluations Derived from Authority. Sometimes the authorities cited in program evaluations are rhetoricians and philosophers from the past who have recognized the importance of writing to thought and even to civilization. Confucius, for example, claimed that good writing is essential for the good of the state, and Thomas Jefferson regarded it as essential to a democracy. In the first chapter of this book, I cited, as an authority, the AAC report on the meaning of the baccalaureate degree. But these authorities—although their claims about the importance of the discipline are convincing—can tell us nothing about the effectiveness of our particular programs. For that measurement, we can ask reputable and experienced authorities in the field of writing to give us their opinions about our programs. The visitor, or team of visitors, can speak to our deans, faculty, and students; the outside experts can compare our instructional design or faculty qualifications or support facilities with those of other institutions. The visiting authorities can then prepare a report evaluating our program.

Such an evaluation—however useful and even convincing— is basically a more or less subjective opinion by an authority or two. Therefore, some empiricists refuse to call it a program evaluation. While I share some of their suspicions, I do not agree that a considered assessment by qualified outside specialists is worthless. I participate regularly in such evaluations and am convinced of their value for any institution that seeks an outside assessment of its program. Sometimes reports by such teams provide support for the most informed faculty and administrators in their efforts to improve a program. But the opinions of authorities cannot yield an evaluation that will be con-

vincing to those who usually rely on data as evidence. Since the
conclusions are normally based on opinion and personal experience rather than institutional data, those who disagree with the
conclusions and remain unimpressed by authority (or the particular authorities involved) have no trouble disregarding the
report.

Evaluations Derived from Intuition. I do not use the
term *intuition* in a mystical sense but, rather, to describe what
we know from our own experience. For example, I know that
my own composition students improve in the course of a term
of study; I know it so completely that if an empirical study
argued that they did not, I would look for flaws in the study
rather than in my teaching. I have seen and experienced student
improvement in my classes for thirty years, and that is felt evidence I will not discard, though I continue to look for ways to
teach more effectively. I trust my intuitions in this regard (and
in many others) absolutely; how could I give final grades, or,
indeed, continue to teach, if I did not? The problem, of course,
is that while I trust my intuitions, I don't have much faith in
yours. Also, I realize that such intuitions do not yield convincing program evaluations.

Evaluations Derived from Deductive Reasoning. It makes
sense, we say, that students who practice a skill will improve,
particularly if they receive expert assessment and advice. Smaller
classes provide better writing instruction, we argue, since individual attention helps students learn better. Since writing and
thinking go together, a good college writing course should contain sophisticated and demanding reading. But we must confess
that these arguments, without some empirical evidence, remain
statements of belief, not proofs, and are convincing only to
those who share our premises. Deductive reasoning cannot by
itself demonstrate that our writing programs are doing what we
claim.

Empirical Evaluations

I have here touched on only a few of the nonempirical
proofs often used as program evaluation. But I must reluctantly
conclude that the only program evaluations likely to seem con-

vincing in an empirical age are in fact empirical. Our funding
agencies and administrations are accustomed to basing their bottom lines on reliable data, and most of us would probably confess in private that we long for the same kind of proof. When
our authorities conflict, our intuitions disagree, and our reasoning leads to diverse conclusions, we long for some evidence that
at least appears to be based on cold, hard facts. Perhaps in these
facts we will find the simple answers to our hard questions.

As Ann Ruggles Gere (1985a) has recently shown, empirical research has been part of composition studies in this country
nearly from their beginning. The tradition began with the first
Harvard report in 1892, assessing English A; flowered in the
1960s with Kitzhaber's study at Dartmouth and the Braddock
team's summary of research; and continues unabated in the
1980s with the studies summarized in this book. Our relatively
new concern for reliability and validity in composition testing
(White, 1985) might even be seen as one tide in this continuing
empirical sea of composition research. Those committed to empirical research, or its ethnographic and clinical offshoots, have
dominated the field and arrogated the very term *research* for
their own particular methodology.

But empirical research in program evaluation has not by
any means given us simple answers or even clear ways of reaching answers to our questions about the effectiveness of writing
programs. Despite its strong appeal as a dominant method of
research, it has not been able to deliver the certainties that we
long for. (See North, 1987, pp. 141–196, for an excellent review
of the method.) I will return shortly to the implications of this
methodology for writing programs in general. In relation to program evaluation, we must simply recognize that there is no
replicated design in existence for demonstrating that any writing instructional program in fact improves student writing, if we
define writing in a sophisticated way. While there are isolated
examples here and there, usually without much statistical sophistication, of some measurable student improvement, we have
not, despite massive efforts, come up with an experimental
model we can point to and say, "Yes, this is how we demonstrate
that student writing has been improved by this particular pro-

gram." Hillocks's (1986) elaborate meta-analysis must be seen as the latest in a series of heroic efforts to achieve some conclusions by this method. Richard Larson's dry question in his review of the book captures the reaction neatly: "After such promise, what fulfillment?" The review provides the expected answer: Not much (Larson, 1987, pp. 207–211).

The most dramatic example of this depressing inability of empirical research to provide us with convincing program evaluation is the fine book published in 1983 by Southern Illinois University Press: Stephen Witte and Lester Faigley's *Evaluating College Writing Programs*. The book has an unintended dramatic structure. In its opening sections, it examines closely a series of empirical program evaluations that failed. The authors select the best empirical precedents and mercilessly detail exactly where these efforts went wrong. At the center of the book is the promise that the authors, who are planning their own program evaluation, will avoid all past errors in their own design. The drama builds as we see the new and more perfect plan they evolve and proceed to implement. And then, the denouement, the reward of hubris, the fate of those who challenge the gods: the even more spectacular failure of the new design, with an assessment of the new and more sophisticated errors they committed. It is hard to know which to admire more—the honesty and writing skill of the authors, as they show that they too have failed at writing program evaluation, or the damnable recalcitrance of the problem they tried in vain to solve.

The nonfinding of this Witte-Faigley study, by the way, replicates the nonresults of the exceedingly well-funded Carnegie Foundation evaluation of the (then) Bay Area Writing Project. That evaluation, headed by Michael Scriven, produced no less than thirty-two separate reports, "none of which," according to the *Carnegie Quarterly*, "was able to present direct cause-and-effect statistics" ("Teaching and Learning the Art of Composition," 1979, p. 7).

To be sure, if we reduce the scope of the problem sufficiently, we can come up with something. Hillocks (1986) summarizes certain kinds of results and, in his meta-analyses, gives certain kinds of confirmation about effective and ineffective teaching "modes" and "foci" in writing programs (see Chapter Three). We can take a small part of writing, such as spelling or syntax, and show that some kinds of classwork can improve scores on certain narrow kinds of tests. We can imagine that T-units are in fact (as they are in some theories) a way of defining writing quality and then show how to lengthen students' T-units. We can use sentence combining to lengthen sentences, and we can drill on active verbs to shorten sentences. We can use error counts, as Kitzhaber's 1963 study at Dartmouth did, to show that freshmen write better than seniors; we can use six-way scoring of complicated essays on three kinds of scales, as the California project (White and Polin, 1986) did, to show that weak student writers perform better on campuses where there are upper-division writing requirements. But we seem always to circle about and get no closer to the "simple" question of whether this or that writing program actually makes students write better or not.

Resistance of Writing Programs to Empirical Evaluation

Despite all this evidence for pessimism, I am going to recommend a plan in this chapter. But before I demonstrate my own hubris in this way, I want to examine the reasons for the resistance of writing programs to the sort of empirical evaluation that seems to work in many other areas.

In the first place, we need to recognize the number of removes from reality that empirical program evaluation requires. There is, on the first level, the student—thinking, learning, daydreaming. On the second level is the written expression of that student's mental activity: a first-draft writing product, a survey of some sort, a demonstration of the writing process, a portfolio of processes and products. Then we have the third remove from reality, the evaluation of that second level. This evaluation may be a number, a letter grade, a statement of some sort, a profile of scores, or any combination. Then comes the fourth level, for we are not here concerned with individuals but with groups: we must aggregate these measures somehow to come up with group measures. Furthermore, we must have comparable group measures over time, for a single group measure can tell us little; we need to compare performance in order to show improvement. But we have seen the perils of pretesting and posttesting. On this treacherous shoal have foundered virtually all the hopeful empirical evaluation barks that have been launched. But yet a further remove into abstraction and metaphor awaits. We must now apply statistical tests of reliability, validity, and significance to whatever group comparative data may still be afloat. Then, and only then, can we measure the probability (*never* in this method the certainty) that our findings are not the result of chance. Only after these tests have battered our work can we stand up and assert that our program has indeed proven itself to be of value. But we can't seem to get the numbers people to perform their psychomagic (as a statistician I know calls it) for us; they usually abandon ship well before we stand naked and alone on the farther shore declaring that our programs work.

But, of course, we and our colleagues have known the value of our work from the beginning of the measurement effort. We know it from our intuition, our experience, our reasoning, even from the opinions of outside authorities. The great frustration of program evaluation in writing is that we *see* students improve, we *know* that they write better, we have all kinds of unofficial nonempirical evidence to show that our programs are valuable.

We thus find ourselves like Dr. Johnson, kicking the stone to demonstrate reality, despite the arguments of the philosophers. But, like the philosophers, the granting agencies and the trustees smile at our naiveté and then award the spoils of statistically demonstrated value elsewhere.

So let us return to the catalogue of problems we face in empirical writing program evaluation. We share the many removes from reality I have just described with some other disciplines; our problem of definition, however, is almost unique. What is this thing that we are measuring, and how do these different meanings affect our comparisons of group performance?

This question returns us to the central problem of defining what we mean by "writing" or "writing skill" or "writing program." Everyone involved with the measurement of writing has faced this problem in one way or another, since we test writing by selecting, as a first step, a relatively narrow definition. For example, the old-fashioned multiple-choice usage tests, despite all the talk of correlation with real writing, defined writing as a particularly picky and social-class-oriented version of error identification. In recent years, we have moved away from those multiple-choice usage tests and their reflection in analytic scoring guides in order to enforce a definition of writing that accords more with the concept of writing as a thinking process. But we know that even among writing teachers there is little agreement on this definition. We are familiar with the reactions of untrained graders of student writing; as we have seen for decades, without agreement on standards all papers get all scores. We have developed holistic or primary-trait scales in order to stipulate definitions, so that we can achieve reasonably reliable scoring of single tests. (For a discussion of the history and the effectiveness of this process, see White, 1985, pp. 18–33, 120–148.) We have learned how, on a single test, to cope with the fact that writing is for some readers a structural concept, for others a stylistic one, for others a mysteriously creative one, for others a conventional or mechanical one, and for still others a moral one. The recent developments in the testing of writing require a clear, focused, and forced agreement on the definition of writing for a particular test.

But our ability to cope with this definitional problem on a test is by no means a sign that we have really solved the problem or that it can be solved or even that it ought to be solved in general. Even though scoring guides, anchor papers, and similar methods to force consensus have put order into our group scoring of tests, a serious attempt at program evaluation throws us back into the primal chaos once more. In this chaos, the multiple and conflicting definitions of writing are both our despair (they keep us from giving simple answers) and our hope; indeed, it is through this complexity of definition that we are likely to find the answers we seek.

Thus, we cannot use our new tools for achieving agreement about writing on essay tests very effectively in the area of program evaluation. We must recognize and allow others to recognize that writing is all the aspects of learning and expression that I have briefly summarized, and more. That is, we need to develop new theories about the meaning of writing for program evaluation purposes—theories that define writing more inclusively than our holistic scoring guides and other testing documents do. For example, a simple pretest/posttest evaluation design, even using sophisticated question development and careful holistic scoring, normally yields no gain scores for groups across an academic year. We know that the students are writing better, but the measurement device does not show it. Why? The reasons have become plain: the relatively small improvement in writing ability that occurs even in a first-rate writing program (when compared with a lifetime of language use) tends not to show up in the rough and relatively unreliable scores of a single test of first-draft writing. Furthermore, many aspects of what has been taught, from revision and editing procedures to reading and library research skills, are not tested by the timed essay. In addition, such a set of tests does not even attempt to look at certain long-range benefits that we sometimes claim for writing, such as intellectual or moral growth, increased ability to learn, and enhanced understanding of the self. We cannot simply import routine test procedures into program evaluation and expect them to yield results. Instead of trimming down what we measure, so that we can measure it accurately, we need to expand our procedures, so that we can catch improvements of all sorts wherever they may show up.

My point here is that we need to think differently about these basic matters when we shift contexts. Program evaluation is not just large-scale writing assessment; it is a wholly different, if related, activity. And if writing assessment is difficult and complex, program evaluation is even more so.

Recommendations

I have three recommendations on the subject. I wish I had more, but since my major conclusion is that we don't really know very much about writing program evaluation, three may be the right number. I certainly don't want to conclude this chapter with a false sense of satisfaction and closure. Here are my recommendations for those embarking on the task: (1) Learn from the past. (2) Use multiple measures. (3) Emphasize formative rather than summative evaluation. My discussion of these recommendations will be very brief.

Learn from the Past. I have mentioned the Hillocks study, the Witte and Faigley book, and the NIE-funded California project (White and Polin, 1986). The team that evaluated the Bay Area Writing Project for the Carnegie Foundation produced a handbook for evaluators, now published in a revised and somewhat enlarged second edition (Davis and others, 1987). No informed evaluation design can afford to ignore the lessons that have emerged from this work. Be aware of the need for careful definitions and the enormous complexity of the enterprise; know that a serious program evaluation will need substantial resources, trained personnel, and ample time for the work. Try hard to avoid the mistakes that your predecessors have committed; be inventive enough to commit your own. Most of all, be aware of the probability of failure, the extreme difficulty of obtaining results. That is, acquire an overriding sense of anxiety and humility.

Use Multiple Measures. If you have adequately learned from the past, you will place many eggs in very many baskets. You will measure everything possible, in the hope that something may possibly work out. You will measure attitudes as well as performance; you will look for long-term as well as short-term effects; you will enlist faculty to conduct ministudies wherever possible. An example of this approach is the evaluation of the writing-across-the-curriculum program in the Minnesota Community College system, 1986-1988. Under the direction of Gail Hughes-Wiener, this wide-ranging assessment has so many pieces that the odds of showing some results are much higher than usual (for the outline of that plan, see Resource A at the back of this book).

Emphasize Formative Rather Than Summative Evaluation. A program evaluation ought to benefit the participants even if it does not, finally, convince its funding source. For example, convening groups of faculty to develop criteria for an evaluation inevitably leads to an exchange of views and a review of goals. A well-conceived scoring session will yield not only reliable test scores but also regular conversation over meals about ways to increase those scores by improved curriculum or teaching. Preparing and scoring a holistic test can lead to improved class essay assignments by participating faculty, and faculty outside of the writing program who are assessing the uses of writing in learning are bound to incorporate writing into their curricula more effectively because of what they themselves learn during the assessment. Even if we do not know how to measure program results very well, we do know how to help teachers teach more effectively. We should be sure that program evaluation supports teaching and becomes a useful part of the program itself. We can in this way ensure that the evaluation effort will be valuable, whatever its results may be.

Empirical Methodology and Knowledge About Composition Programs

The problems with empirical methodology that I have been alluding to are worth further discussion, because they lead us back to the central questions of this book: How can we improve composition programs to the point that they can justify their claim to a position at the center of postsecondary education? How can a concerned faculty and administration improve significantly the campus climate for writing, and thus for thinking and learning? If our most trusted means of generating information—that is, the inductive reasoning and empirical methodology that have led to modern science and technology—will not reliably confirm the value of writing programs, can we really believe that writing does what we claim?

One response to these perplexities is to return to Einstein: "Everything should be as simple as possible—but no simpler." Empirical methodologies require relatively uncomplicated and clear phenomena, so that experiments can be run with sufficient controls. If the phenomenon we are studying is complicated, we need to isolate one or two variables for examination while we hold everything else constant. Furthermore, the method is more attuned to what North (1987, p. 145) calls *"discon-firming* possible explanations" than to discovery of truth; since empiricism must leap to generalizations from a limited number of cases, it confirms theories by failing to deny them, and its inferences must always be tentative. In addition, a kind of positivism lies behind the empirical quest: the world is assumed to be orderly, definable, and knowable. When the investigator discovers the rules that govern the world, they hold in all similar cases; thus, empirical experiments must be replicable if they reveal truth.

The nature of writing and the nature of writing programs certainly seem ill suited for this kind of inquiry. While any sensible person must grant empirical inquiry enormous power in the investigation of the physical world, it is not necessarily the best method for inquiry into either the process or the success of writing programs. Certainly, the results of empirical program evaluation are discouraging—as, indeed, are the results of empirical research in writing in general: an enormous investment of time, energy, and money has produced mainly survey data, tending to organize what every thoughtful person knew all along.

In program evaluation, as in all other aspects of writing programs, we need to resist using or accepting simple and reductive definitions, procedures, tests, and inferences. It is surely a wise instinct that leads us to trust writing instruction more to poets than to scientists, or even to logicians. The resistant reality of learning to think, to write, to create, to revise and recreate, to understand, does not yield its secrets readily. Our primary job, in program evaluation as in many other aspects of our work, is to help others see the complexity and importance of writing, to distinguish between the simple and the not so simple, to be willing to accept the evidence of many kinds of serious inquiry into the nature of creative thought. That, of course, is just one more way of defining the function of every teacher and every scholar.

Resource A

Evaluation of
the Writing-Across-
the-Curriculum Program—
Minnesota Community
College System

(Funded by a grant from the Bush Foundation)
Gail Hughes-Wiener, Program Evaluator

**GOAL 1: Increase the Amount and Types of
Student Writing Done Across the Curriculum**

**GOAL 2: Improve Faculty Attitudes Towards
the Use of Writing in Instruction**

Evaluation Devices for These Goals

> *Faculty Evaluation of the WAC Program:* End-of-year
> Likert-Scale survey of all WAC faculty
> *Hour-Long Interviews* of a random sample of WAC faculty

GOAL 3: Increase the Quality of Student Writing

> *Holistic Rating of Student Essays* gathered in a random
> sample of WAC classrooms; essay ratings will be corre-
> lated with participation in WAC classes

GOAL 4: Increase Student Attainment of Subject Goals Through Instructional Writing

Quasi-Experimental "Matched Classes" Studies (in most cases, two sections of the same class; use of Holistic Subject Rating to score essay exams)

GOAL 5: Improve Student Attitudes Towards Writing

Course Evaluation Survey by students in both Experimental and Control classes

Student Evaluation of Writing Activities Survey by students in Experimental classes

GOAL 6: Provide Information for Organizing WAC Workshops

Workshop Checklist: All participants complete a survey in which they rate workshop sessions

Short-Answer Questionnaire completed by workshop participants several weeks after returning to their campuses

GOAL 7: Provide Information for Organizing Follow-Up Activities

Background Characteristics Survey (reasons for attending and previous experiences with writing activities)

Writing Issues Survey (short pre- and post-workshop survey)

Information Needs Survey (short end-of-workshop survey)

GOAL 8: Provide Diagnostic Information Which Will Enable Faculty to Be More Effective in Their Use of Writing Activities

Teaching Strategy Form by Experimental teachers

Writing Activities Diagnosis Form by Experimental teachers

Resource B

Guidelines for Self-Study to Precede a Writing Program Evaluation

Council of Writing Program Administrators

At least one month before the WPA consultant-evaluators are scheduled to visit your campus, you should prepare a self-study to acquaint consultants with your institution. The self-study should be largely a narrative report, addressing the concerns enumerated below. You need not answer all of these questions, but you should address yourself to those issues which will give the consultants a clear view of the history of your program. **The final self-study should be about 10 pages in length, not including any charts or supporting documents.**

I. Focus of the Evaluation Visit
- A. What are the program's current concerns? What questions would you like to see the evaluators address?
- B. What changes (if any) is the program planning to implement?

II. Curriculum
- A. Philosophy and Goals
  1. What are the principles or philosophy of the writing program(s) at your institution?
  2. What are the goals of the writing program(s)?

How do these goals reflect the program's philosophy?

3. How were the philosophy and goals developed, and how are they currently articulated?

4. What goals do the administration and faculty in other departments think that the writing program should have? How do the goals of the writing program accord with the goals of the institution as a whole?

B. Courses and Syllabuses

1. What writing courses are currently taught? In the English Department? Elsewhere in the institution?

2. How are these courses related? Are they required? If so, of whom? What are their prerequisites?

3. Does your institution incorporate and reinforce writing throughout the curriculum? How?

4. How are the needs of ESL students addressed? How are the needs of basic writers addressed?

5. Does each writing course have a syllabus? Are the syllabuses uniform or individual?

6. If your syllabuses are uniform, what opportunities exist for experimentation? If your syllabuses are individual, what is the principle of coherence across the sections?

7. Is there a logical sequence of assignments within each course? How does each syllabus relate to program goals and institutional goals?

8. Are there opportunities for faculty to share and develop syllabuses? What control does the writing program administrator have over syllabuses and their development?

9. How much writing, and what kind of writing, must students do for each course? What role does revision play?

10. How much reading is assigned in writing courses? What is the purpose or function of reading assigned in the writing courses?

C. Instructional Methods and Materials

1. What instructional methods are used in the program's writing courses? What kinds of classroom activities are most common?

2. Do the writing courses use textbooks? How many and what kind (handbooks, rhetorics, anthologies, workbooks, dictionaries, etc.)? Which books are used in which courses? Who makes decisions about texts? What options are available for faculty and for teaching assistants or adjunct faculty? Why is the program using the textbooks it is currently using? What instructional materials and media does the program use other than textbooks?

3. How is student writing incorporated into the instructional material? What kind of reproduction facilities are available to duplicate student work for classes? Are they readily available?

4. How much time do instructors devote to individual conferences? Do they all have adequate office space for conferences with students?

D. Responses to and Assessment of Student Writing

1. At what stages do students receive responses to their writing?

2. How do faculty members evaluate student writing? What criteria and procedures are used?

3. How are grades determined in individual

courses? Are there agreed-upon criteria? How does the program arrive at uniformity in grading across sections?

E.   Testing

    1.   What tests and testing procedures does the program currently use for placement and exemption? Why were these particular tests chosen? Have they been validated for the population of students they are administered to at this institution? When were they last evaluated?

    2.   How are placement decisions made and carried out? Does the program evaluate proficiency? If so, how does this evaluation relate to the philosophy and goals of the program?

    3.   How are the tests administered? Who administers them? Who scores them? How are those who administer and score tests compensated?

    4.   What is the program's policy on testing and placing transfer students?

III.   Program Administration

A.   Institutional and Program Structure

    1.   What writing programs are there on campus? Freshman composition? Writing across the curriculum? Technical writing?

    2.   What is the size and make-up of each of the departments or administrative units in which these programs are housed? What is the governing structure of each?

    3.   What is the internal governing structure of the writing program? Is there a writing program administrator ("director of freshman English," "composition committee chair," "ESL director," etc.)? If so, what is the WPA's administrative relation to other levels of administration? To whom is the WPA re-

sponsible? Who decides the WPA's tenure, promotion, and salary?

4. How is the writing program related through administration and curriculum to other departments and divisions in the institution?

5. If there are night school or nondegree programs, who determines how writing is taught in those programs? How is that control exercised? Who is responsible for the teaching of writing in other departments or colleges within the institution?

6. How is the teaching of writing funded? Who controls these funds? On what are these funds spent? How does the funding of the writing program compare to the funding of other programs on campus?

7. Who hires, promotes, and tenures the writing staff? Who determines their salaries and assigns courses to them?

8. How are new teaching positions determined, and by whom?

9. Who determines class size, curriculum, and teaching load?

10. How are internal problems solved? Who decides on syllabuses, testing procedures, textbooks, curriculum, etc.? What voice do full-time faculty, part-time faculty, teaching assistants, and students have in shaping policies?

11. What permanent or *ad hoc* committees relevant to the teaching of writing exist? How are these committees appointed? What do they do?

12. What are the procedures for negotiating student and faculty complaints about grading, teaching, and administrative processes and policies?

           13. What administrative and clerical support is there?

  B. Writing Program Administrator(s)

    1. How is the WPA chosen?

    2. What are the terms and conditions of appointment of the WPA? What are the academic and professional qualifications of the WPA? What is the WPA's rank and tenure status? What is the WPA's teaching load? How much research is the WPA expected to do? Of what type? What is the length of the WPA's appointment? How is the WPA's work (administrative, teaching, research) evaluated? By whom? How is the WPA rewarded? Are the terms and conditions of the WPA's appointment in writing?

IV. Faculty

  A. Status and Working Conditions

    1. What percentage of full-time faculty at each rank, adjunct faculty, and graduate students teach writing? How many writing courses do faculty at each rank or status teach?

    2. What are the qualifications for writing faculty and how are they established? What training and experience do writing faculty have? What professional organizations do they belong to? What is their record of research, publication, conference participation, and professional activity?

    3. What are the salary ranges by rank and category? How do these salary ranges compare to comparable departments? To neighboring, comparable institutions?

    4. How are teaching and research rewarded in terms of salary, promotion, and tenure?

    5. How are adjunct faculty appointed? By whom? When in relation to the opening of

a term? How are the adjunct faculty compensated in terms of salary and benefits? Are there step raises or cost of living increases for adjunct faculty? Are adjunct faculty compensated for preparation if a course does not fill or is covered by a full-time faculty member? Is there a departmental policy on percentage of part-time faculty? Do adjunct faculty attend department meetings and writing program meetings? What opportunities exist for adjunct faculty to develop curriculum, choose textbooks, formulate policy and procedures? What arrangements are made for office space, telephones, mailboxes, and clerical support for adjunct faculty?

B. Faculty Development

1. How is faculty development defined as a goal of the institution, the department or administrative unit, and the writing program? What are ongoing plans for faculty development?

2. What courses, speaker programs, workshops, teaching awards, and support series does the program offer or support to encourage excellence in teaching writing?

3. What opportunities for faculty development already exist? Who uses them? How do faculty find out about them? In what ways are faculty encouraged to avail themselves of these opportunities?

4. Are these opportunities available to faculty who hold other than full-time, continuing, tenure-track appointments?

5. What kinds of work and activities occur during department or program staff meetings? How frequently are these meetings held? Who attends them?

6.   What financial resources are available for travel to workshops, conferences, and institutes?

7.   What avenues exist for writing faculty at each rank and status to design, implement, and evaluate faculty development programs best suited to their needs and interests? How are faculty encouraged to develop their skills in composition research and teaching writing? What opportunities exist for learning about faculty development programs at other institutions?

8.   Does the department or institution support faculty by offering leaves of absence for further education, publishing in journals, developing software or other media, articulation with high schools, or articulation with community organizations?

9.   What support does the department or institution give for development of institutional and individual grants and for released time, overhead, and other support to carry out the grant?

V.   Related Programs and Services

This section includes questions that pertain to any academic or service program that relates to writing instruction for any student in the institution. Examples would include: a writing center, a reading lab, a learning center, a test center, library workshops, tutoring services, and ESL programs. Each service or program should be considered in light of the following concerns.

A.   Organization

1.   Describe the services or programs at the institution that enhance the teaching of writing. Focus on services offered, goals, clientele, and pedagogy.

2.   What kinds of materials (books, computers) and techniques (tutoring, workshops) does each service use?

3. To what extent do the faculty and students in the writing program and elsewhere in the institution know that these services exist? What is the faculty attitude toward these services? Do they refer students there or use the services themselves?

4. How many students and which faculty use this service? What is the profile of students who use each service?

5. How are students placed in or referred to each support service? Is there any reciprocal communication?

B. Personnel

1. What are the qualifications for positions in the support service? How are the director and staff selected? What is the institutional status (faculty, graduate student, full-time, part-time, etc.) of support service personnel? How are they compensated for their work? How is their work evaluated?

2. How are support service personnel trained?

3. What opportunities are there for professional development of support service personnel? How does the institution reward support service personnel for improving the service and for developing themselves professionally?

4. What kind of relationship exists between the writing program faculty and support service personnel? Do writing program faculty and support service personnel meet regularly to discuss students involved in both programs? Is there an active exchange of information on curricular and administrative matters?

C. Administration

1. Do students get credit for work completed in support services? If so, how is credit determined?

2. How is each support service funded? Who decides how the money is spent? How is it currently being spent?
3. Does each support service follow up on students who have used its services?
4. Is there continuing self-evaluation of each service by its staff? Is each service regularly evaluated by someone not actively involved in its work?
5. Do any services offered by the writing program and the support services overlap? Do their common goals and procedures reinforce each other or conflict? In what formal or informal ways (through scheduling, a coordinating committee, etc.) is each support service coordinated with the writing program?

D. Outreach Programs

What kind(s) of programs does the college or university provide that are connected with secondary schools, professional schools, or community writing programs?

You do not want to overwhelm consultants with background materials, but you may want to include the following in an appendix to the narrative report.

1. Statistical information for the previous and current academic year: enrollments, class sizes, composition of the teaching staff, final grade distribution.
2. A description of each course within the program(s) to be evaluated (objectives, syllabuses, texts, placement and exemption procedures, grading criteria).
3. Copies of evaluative instruments.
4. Materials pertaining to teacher training (both faculty and graduate students or adjuncts), including orientation meeting agendas, workshop description, and syllabuses for training courses.

5. School catalogues, department handbooks, and depart-
    mental student materials.

Send these materials to:

Professor Edward M. White
Department of English
California State University
San Bernardino, CA 92407

References

Applebee, A. N. *Tradition and Reform in the Teaching of English: A History.* Urbana, Ill.: National Council of Teachers of English, 1974.

Applebee, A. N. *Writing in the Secondary School: English and the Content Areas.* Urbana, Ill.: National Council of Teachers of English, 1981.

Association of American Colleges. "Integrity in the College Curriculum: A Report to the Academic Community." *Chronicle of Higher Education,* Feb. 13, 1985, *29* (22), 12–30.

Bain, A. *English Composition and Rhetoric.* New York: Appleton-Century-Crofts, 1866.

Bereiter, C., and Scardamalia, M. "Levels of Inquiry in Writing Research." In P. Mosenthal and others (eds.), *Research on Writing.* New York: Longman, 1983.

Berkenkotter, C., and Murray, D. "Decisions and Revisions: The Planning Strategies of a Publishing Writer, and Response of a Laboratory Rat—Or, Being Protocoled." *College Composition and Communication,* 1983, *34,* 156–172.

Bizzell, P. "What Can We Know, What Must We Do, What May We Hope: Writing Assessment." *College English,* 1987, *49* (5), 575–584.

Blackmur, R. P. "Toward a Modus Vivendi." In *The Lion and*

the Honeycomb: Essays in Solicitude and Critique. San Diego, Calif.: Harcourt Brace Jovanovich, 1955.

Bloom, B., and others. *Handbook on Formative and Summative Evaluation of Student Learning.* New York: McGraw-Hill, 1971.

Braddock, R., Lloyd-Jones, R., and Schoer, L. *Research in Written Composition.* Urbana, Ill.: National Council of Teachers of English, 1963.

Bray, J., and others. *New Directions for State Teacher Policies.* No. TR-85-1. Denver: Education Commission of the States, 1985.

Breland, H., and others. *Assessing Writing Skill.* New York: College Entrance Examination Board, 1987.

Britton, J., and others. *The Development of Writing Abilities (11–18).* New York: Macmillan, 1975.

Brown, R. "Evaluation and Learning." In *The Teaching of Writing: Eighty-Fifth Yearbook of the National Society for the Study of Education.* Chicago: National Society for the Study of Education, 1986.

Chapman, D. W., and Tate, G. "A Survey of Doctoral Programs in Rhetoric and Composition." *Rhetoric Review,* Spring 1987, *5* (2), 124–186.

Clark, I. *Writing in the Center: Teaching in a Writing Center Setting.* Dubuque, Iowa: Kendall/Hunt, 1985.

Comprone, J. J. "Literary Theory and Composition." In G. Tate (ed.), *Teaching Composition: 12 Bibliographical Essays.* Fort Worth: Texas Christian University Press, 1987.

Connolly, P., and Vilardi, T. *New Methods in College Writing Programs: Theories in Practice.* New York: Modern Language Association, 1986.

Connors, R. "Composition Studies and Science." *College English,* 1983, *45,* 1–20.

Cooper, C., and Odell, L. (eds.). *Research on Composing: Points of Departure.* Urbana, Ill.: National Council of Teachers of English, 1978.

D'Angelo, F. J. "Aims, Modes, and Forms of Discourse." In G. Tate (ed.), *Teaching Composition: 12 Bibliographical Essays.* Fort Worth: Texas Christian University Press, 1987.

Davis, B. G., and others. *The Evaluation of Composition Instruction.* (2nd ed.) New York: Teachers College Press, 1987.

Denham, R. D. "From the Editor." *Association of Departments of English Bulletin,* Fall 1987, No. 87, pp. i–iv.

Diederich, P. *Measuring Growth in English.* Urbana, Ill.: National Council of Teachers of English, 1974.

Durst, R. K. "Books: *Research on Written Composition.*" *The Quarterly* (National Writing Project and Center for the Study of Writing, University of California, Berkeley), 1987, *9* (3), 23–25.

Elbow, P. *Writing Without Teachers.* New York: Oxford University Press, 1973.

Emig, J. *The Composing Processes of Twelfth Graders.* Urbana, Ill.: National Council of Teachers of English, 1971.

Faigley, L., and others. *Assessing Writers' Knowledge and Processes of Composing.* Norwood, N.J.: Ablex, 1985.

Flakus-Mosqueda, P. *Survey of States' Teacher Policies.* Denver: Education Commission of the States, 1983.

Fortune, R. (ed.). *School-College Collaborative Programs in English.* New York: Modern Language Association, 1986.

Garrison, R. *How a Writer Works.* New York: Harper & Row, 1981.

Gere, A. R. "Empirical Research in Composition." In B. W. McClelland and T. R. Donovan (eds.), *Perspectives on Research and Scholarship in Composition.* New York: Modern Language Association, 1985a.

Gere, A. R. (ed.). *Roots in the Sawdust: Writing to Learn Across the Disciplines.* Urbana, Ill.: National Council of Teachers of English, 1985b.

Giroux, H. A. "Literacy, Ideology, and the Culture of Schooling." *Humanities in Society,* 1981, *4,* 335–362.

Gould, C., and Heyda, J. "Literacy Education and the Basic Writer: A Survey of College Composition Courses." *Journal of Basic Writing,* 1986, *5* (2), 8–27.

Greenberg, K., Wiener, H., and Donovan, R. *Writing Assessment: Issues and Strategies.* New York: Longman, 1986.

Hairston, M. "The Winds of Change: Thomas Kuhn and the

Revolution in the Teaching of Writing." *College Composition and Communication,* 1982, *33,* 78–86.

Hairston, M. "Breaking Our Bonds and Reaffirming Our Connections." *College Composition and Communication,* 1985, *36,* 272–282.

Harned, J. "The Intellectual Background of Alexander Bain's 'Modes of Discourse.'" *College Composition and Communication,* 1985, *36,* 42–50.

Hartzog, C. P. *Composition and the Academy: A Study of Writing Program Administration.* New York: Modern Language Association, 1986.

Haviland, C. "Writing Centers and Writing-Across-the-Curriculum: An Important Connection." *Writing Center Journal,* 1985, *5,* 25–30.

Heller, S. " 'A Room of Our Own': Association of Composition Researchers Evolves with the Field." *Chronicle of Higher Education,* April 27, 1988, *34* (33), A7.

Hillocks, G., Jr. *Research on Written Composition: New Directions for Teaching.* Urbana, Ill.: National Council of Teachers of English, 1986.

Hirsch, E. D. *Cultural Literacy: What Every American Needs to Know.* Boston: Houghton Mifflin, 1987.

Horner, W. B. (ed.). *Composition and Literature: Bridging the Gap.* Chicago: University of Chicago Press, 1983.

Huber, B. J. (ed.). *A Report on the 1986 Survey of English Doctoral Programs in Writing and Literature.* New York: Modern Language Association, 1988.

Kern, A. "Basic Writing: The Student as Programmer." *Association of Departments of English Bulletin,* Spring 1987, No. 86, p. 4.

Kinneavy, J. *A Theory of Discourse.* Englewood Cliffs, N.J.: Prentice-Hall, 1971.

Kitzhaber, A. R. *Themes, Theories, and Therapy: The Teaching of Writing in College.* New York: McGraw-Hill, 1963.

Knoblauch, C. H. "The Current-Traditional Paradigm: Neither Current, nor Traditional, nor a Paradigm." Paper presented at annual meeting of the Modern Language Association, Chicago, 1985.

Koch, K. *Wishes, Lies and Dreams: Teaching Children to Write Poetry.* New York: Chelsea House, 1970.

Koenig, J., and Mitchell, K. "An Interim Report on the MCAT Essay Pilot Project." *Journal of Medical Education,* 1988, *63,* 21–29.

Krashen, S., Scarcella, R., and Long, M. (eds.). *Child-Adult Differences in Second Language Acquisition.* Rowley, Mass.: Newbury House, 1982.

Larson, R. L. "Review: *Research on Written Composition.*" *College Composition and Communication,* 1987, *38* (2), 207–211.

Levine, K. "Functional Literacy: Fond Illusions and False Economies." *Harvard Educational Review,* 1982, *52,* 249–266.

Lindemann, E. *A Rhetoric for Writing Teachers.* New York: Oxford University Press, 1982.

McCarthy, M. *Memories of a Catholic Girlhood.* San Diego, Calif.: Harcourt Brace Jovanovich, 1957.

McQuade, D. "Who Do You Think You're Talking To?: Trading Ideas for Insults in the English Profession." *English Journal,* 1976, *65,* 8–10.

Maeroff, G. *School and College: Partnerships in Education.* Princeton, N.J.: Carnegie Foundation for the Advancement of Teaching, 1983.

Maimon, E. "The Writing Program at Beaver College." *Forum,* Winter 1981, *2,* 83, 95.

Marchese, T. "Assessment of Basic Skills in Higher Education." Paper presented at National Evaluation Systems Conference, Chicago, Oct. 23, 1987.

Mitchell, K., and Anderson, J. "Reliability of Holistic Scoring for the MCAT Essay." *Educational and Psychological Measurement,* 1986, *46,* 771–775.

Murphy, J. J. (ed.). *The Rhetorical Tradition and Modern Writing.* New York: Modern Language Association, 1982.

North, S. "The Idea of a Writing Center." *College English,* 1984, *46* (5), 433–446.

North, S. *The Making of Knowledge in Composition: Portrait of an Emerging Field.* Upper Montclair, N.J.: Boynton Cook, 1987.

Ohmann, R. M. *English in America: A Radical View of the Profession.* New York: Oxford University Press, 1976.

Ohmann, R. M. "Use Definite, Specific, Concrete Language." *College English*, 1979, *41*, 390–397.

Pattison, R. "The Stupidity Crisis." *Association of Departments of English Bulletin*, Spring 1988, No. 89, pp. 3–10.

Poston, L. "Putting Literacy at the Center." *Association of Departments of English Bulletin*, Winter 1986, No. 85, pp. 13–20.

Robertson, L. R., and Slevin, J. F. "The Status of Composition Faculty: Resolving Reforms." *Rhetoric Review*, Spring 1987, *5* (2), 190–194.

Rose, M. "Remedial Writing Courses: A Critique and a Proposal." *College English*, 1983, *45*, 109–128.

Russell, D. R. "Romantics on Writing: Liberal Culture and the Abolition of Composition Courses." *Rhetoric Review*, Spring 1988, *6* (2), 132–148.

Ruth, L., and Murphy, S. *Designing Writing Tasks for the Assessment of Writing.* Norwood, N.J.: Ablex, 1988.

Scholes, R. *Textual Power: Literacy Theory and the Teaching of English.* New Haven, Conn.: Yale University Press, 1985.

Schultz, L., and others. "Interaction Among School and College Writing Teachers: Toward Recognizing and Remaking Old Patterns." *College Composition and Communication*, 1988, *39* (2), 139–153.

Shale, D. "Essay Reliability: Form and Meaning." Paper presented at annual meeting of the American Educational Research Association, San Francisco, April 1986.

Sommers, N. "Responding to Student Writing." *College Composition and Communication*, 1982, *33*, 148–156.

Tate, G. (ed.). *Teaching Writing: 12 Bibliographical Essays.* Fort Worth: Texas Christian University Press, 1987.

"Teaching and Learning the Art of Composition: The Bay Area Writing Project." *Carnegie Quarterly*, 1979, *27* (2), 7.

Walvoord, B. *Helping Students Write Well: A Guide for Teachers in All Disciplines.* (2nd ed.) New York: Modern Language Association, 1986.

White, E. M. "Post-Structural Literary Criticism and Response to Student Writing." *College Composition and Communication*, 1984, *35*, 186–195.

White, E. M. *Teaching and Assessing Writing: Recent Advances in Understanding, Evaluating, and Improving Student Performance.* San Francisco: Jossey-Bass, 1985.

White, E. M., and Polin, L. *Research in Effective Teaching of Writing: Final Report.* (2 vols.) Washington, D.C.: National Institute of Education, 1986. (Document no. ED 275 007, available through ERIC Document Reproduction Service, 3900 Wheeler Ave., Alexandria, Va. 22304, telephone 800-227-3742.)

Wilcox, T. W. *The Anatomy of College English.* San Francisco: Jossey-Bass, 1973.

Witte, S. "Pre-Text and Composing." *College Composition and Communication*, 1987a, *38* (4), 397–425.

Witte, S. "Review: *Research on Written Composition.*" *College Composition and Communication*, 1987b, *38* (2), 202–207.

Witte, S., and Faigley, L. *Evaluating College Writing Programs.* Carbondale: Southern Illinois University Press, 1983.

Witte, S., and others. *A National Survey of College and University Writing Program Directors.* Technical Report no. 2. Austin: Writing Program Assessment Project, University of Texas, 1981.

Young, R. E. "Paradigms and Problems: Needed Research in Rhetorical Invention." In C. Cooper and L. Odell (eds.), *Research on Composing: Points of Departure.* Urbana, Ill.: National Council of Teachers of English, 1978.

Young, R. E., Becker, A. L., and Pike, K. L. *Rhetoric: Discovery and Change.* San Diego, Calif.: Harcourt Brace Jovanovich, 1970.

Index

A

Ablex, 171
Admissions evaluation, 115–117
Advanced Placement Program, 120–121
American Association for Higher Education, 183
American Association of University Professors, 160
American College Testing Program, 114
American Council on Education, 122
Anderson, J., 116
Applebee, A., 188
Association of American Colleges, 2, 4, 196
Association of American Medical Colleges, 116
Association of American Universities, 31
Association of Departments of English, 159, 186
Astin, A., 49
Austin (Texas) study. *See* Witte, S.

B

Bain, A., 51
Bay Area Writing Project, 38, 177, 199. *See also* National Writing Project
Becker, A., 51
Behavioral objectives, 132
Bennett, W., 95
Bereiter, C., 172
Berkenkotter, C., 16
Bizzell, P., 64–65
Blackmur, R. P., 63
Bloom, B., 131
Braddock, R., 55, 74, 198
Bray, J., 182
Breland, H., 95
Britton, J., 68, 188
Brown, R., 91, 113
Bush Foundation, 147, 207

C

California Basic Educational Skills Test, 183, 185
California State University, 24, 38, 142, 192; English Equivalency Examination, 121–122; teacher certification procedure, 181, 185
California study. *See Research in Effective Teaching of Writing*
Campus climate for writing, 1, 8, 32, 164, 205; and English department, 9; and faculty development, 149; role of central administration in, 13